D0426532

The Gift of Fire

Also by Dan Caro

"NO-HAND" DAN COMPILATION, VOLUME 1
(CD; available at: www.dancaro.com)

Other Hay House Books with Steve Erwin

LED BY FAITH:
Rising from the Ashes of the Rwandan Genocide,
by Immaculée Ilibagiza, with Steve Erwin

LEFT TO TELL:
Discovering God Amidst the Rwandan Holocaust,
by Immaculée Ilibagiza, with Steve Erwin

OUR LADY OF KIBEHO:
Mary Speaks to the World from the Heart of Africa,
by Immaculée Ilibagiza, with Steve Erwin

Please visit:

Hay House USA: **www.hayhouse.com**®
Hay House Australia: **www.hayhouse.com.au**
Hay House UK: **www.hayhouse.co.uk**
Hay House South Africa: **www.hayhouse.co.za**
Hay House India: **www.hayhouse.co.in**

The Gift of Fire

How I Made *Adversity* Work for Me

DAN CARO WITH STEVE ERWIN

HAY HOUSE, INC.
Carlsbad, California • New York City
London • Sydney • Johannesburg
Vancouver • Hong Kong • New Delhi

Published and distributed in the United States by: Hay House, Inc.:
www.hayhouse.com • *Published and distributed in Australia by:*
Hay House Australia Pty. Ltd.: www.hayhouse.com.au • *Published
and distributed in the United Kingdom by:* Hay House UK, Ltd.: www
.hayhouse.co.uk • *Published and distributed in the Republic of South
Africa by:* Hay House SA (Pty), Ltd.: www.hayhouse.co.za • *Distributed
in Canada by:* Raincoast: www.raincoast.com • *Published in India by:*
Hay House Publishers India: www.hayhouse.co.in

Editorial supervision: Jill Kramer • *Project editor:* Shannon Littrell
Design: Riann Bender • *Interior photos:* Courtesy of the author, unless
otherwise noted

Certain names have been changed to protect individuals' privacy.

The author of this book does not dispense medical advice or
prescribe the use of any technique as a form of treatment for physical,
emotional, or medical problems without the advice of a physician,
either directly or indirectly. The intent of the author is only to offer
information of a general nature to help you in your quest for emotional
and spiritual well-being. In the event you use any of the information
in this book for yourself, which is your constitutional right, the author
and the publisher assume no responsibility for your actions.

Library of Congress Cataloging-in-Publication Data

Caro, Dan.
  The gift of fire : how I made adversity work for me / Dan Caro with
Steve Erwin. -- 1st ed.
       p. cm.
  ISBN 978-1-4019-2660-1 (hardcover)
  1. Caro, Dan, 1979- 2. Burns and scalds--Patients--Louisiana--New
Orleans Region--Biography. 3. Burns and scalds--Patients--Rehabil-
itation. 4. Jazz musicians--Louisiana--New Orleans Region--Biogra-
phy. 5. Drummers (Musicians)--Louisiana--New Orleans--Biography.
6. New Orleans Region (La.)--Biography. I. Erwin, Steve. II. Title.
  RD96.4.C373 2010
  617.1'1092--dc22
  [B]
                                            2009049490

ISBN: 978-1-4019-2660-1

13 12 11 10   4 3 2 1
1st edition, March 2010

Printed in the United States of America

For my parents, John and Marilyn—
the strongest souls I've ever known.

Contents

Foreword

You are about to read a book that will forever change your concept of the word *impossible.*

Dan Caro's story will introduce you to a whole new way of looking at the power of the human spirit. Somewhere within the soul of this young man, there exists a kind of magical vision that has allowed him to overcome the most challenging and difficult set of circumstances and emerge as a role model for all of us. This inner vision not only made a survivor out of Dan, but it has given him the ability to live his life at a level that most people—especially those who have never been confronted by such challenges—couldn't even imagine for themselves.

When I first heard about all that Dan had been through, I was deeply and profoundly moved by his unwillingness to make excuses for anything in his life . . . and God knows he certainly would have been forgiven had he not made that choice. Had Dan just given up after being terribly burned as a two-year-old, everyone would have understood and explained it away as the natural result of a horrifying accident. But in some mysterious way, he simply refused to travel that road. Instead, he calls what happened to him his "gift of fire," and he has made his life an example for all of us to admire and attempt to emulate.

I met Dan as I was making preparations for a national PBS special based on my book *Excuses Begone!* I immediately asked him to come on board with me and provide a firsthand, live example of someone overcoming enormous adversity *sans* any and all excuse making. Dan rocked the audience and absolutely blew me away, giving a stirring performance of how to be a world-class drummer without the benefit of hands.

Dan is one of the most inspirational people I have ever had the privilege of meeting. I love his message, and I love the man even more. I know that his story will not only fill *you* with admiration for his truly remarkable achievements over the past 28 years, but it will also help you realize the truth in the old maxim: "Nothing is impossible to a determined soul."

I encouraged Dan to write this book after receiving thousands of letters from people who told me how much inspiration they received from watching him on my PBS special. I love the beautifully honest rendition he's given of his life in these pages. Yet nothing written here (or anywhere) can begin to depict the soul of Dan Caro. His determination and courage leave me in awe, and his sense of humor about it all leaves me breathless. His original title for his book was *Look, Ma, No Hands!* That says a lot about the character of my friend Dan Caro, about whom I say, "Look, everyone, no excuses!"

— **Dr. Wayne W. Dyer**
Maui, Hawaii

♦ ♦ ♦

Chapter One

Birth, Death, and Rebirth

I was born just a stone's throw from the Big Easy. My mother gave birth to me in the heart of bayou country—in the old southeastern Louisiana town of Metairie. That's right outside the one and only city of New Orleans.

There are two things you can't escape in New Orleans: the humidity and the music. If you're lucky enough to call this place home, the humidity is a burden you learn to live with, and the music is a penetrating joy you never want to go too long without. And if you're a musician—especially a jazz drummer—what better place to grow up than the birthplace of jazz itself?

New Orleans has its own cadence, a rhythm fashioned centuries ago amidst the cultural clash of its first inhabitants and the subsequent blending of African, European, and Latin musical traditions. What evolved

1

was a rhythm that is distinctively American, and as primitive and potent as the human heartbeat. It's a rhythm that has given birth to countless new harmonious styles, from jazz to zydeco, from Cajun music to the Delta Blues. It's an inherently soulful sound that has endured wars and disease, hurricanes and floods. But it's also woven into the tapestry of daily life in the Big Easy, part of everything from funeral processions to prayer meetings, from garage jam sessions to smoke-filled Bourbon Street jazz clubs, from the smallest music festival to Mardi Gras itself.

That rhythm pulled my soul to the city before I was born, wooed the cosmos when I was only an embryonic notion to my parents—and, as I emerged, planted a vision in my heart and body that I'd follow for my life to come.

Yes, I believe I was destined to become a musician. So I was not in the least surprised to learn that my parents, John and Marilyn, had met and fallen in love at a concert. Both of my father's parents had played musical instruments, and Dad was a professional musician himself in his younger years and had even managed to support himself playing the trumpet. Unfortunately, as I would one day discover, being a musician is a precarious career at best, and paychecks can be few and far between. So when my parents decided to get married, Dad put the trumpet aside and began selling insurance.

Soon my mother and father had saved enough money to buy a small house in a lower-middle-income neighborhood in Metairie and begin raising a family. When I arrived in the world on November 16, 1979, the Caro family was already well under way. My eldest brother,

John Jr. (or Johnny, as we all call him), was born seven years before me and was an only child for four years until my brother Scott arrived on the scene. For most of my seminal years I was the baby of the family, a role I was forced to give up when my little brother, Paul, was born not long after my eighth birthday.

We weren't wealthy by any stretch of the imagination, but to use a cliché that truly fit our family life, we were "rich in love." We lived modestly but never wanted for anything. We always owned the house we lived in, and that house was constantly filled with laughter and music. Friends, relatives, and neighbors crowded our backyard during countless barbeques. And although I honestly don't know how my parents afforded it, every year without fail they packed my three brothers and me (and usually a couple of our pals) into the family van and drove us somewhere exotic—such as the Florida Panhandle—for a summer vacation. We'd fish, sail, and enjoy days of doing nothing but exploring sandy beaches and plunging into the warm waters of the Gulf of Mexico.

Curiously, my very first memory is when I was only three or four months old. My big brother Johnny picked me up and held me over a small brick pond in our backyard so that I could see the goldfish that lived there. The shiny orange fish apparently fascinated me, and Johnny held me above the water as I giggled. Even though I was being dangled perilously over water, there is nothing terrifying in that memory for me now—just a sense of contentment while being in the arms of someone who loved me. And despite the trauma my family would endure less than two short years later, that feeling of being protected by every member of my family throughout my childhood is one of the things I treasure most even now.

I also grew up secure in the belief that there was a higher power watching over me. My parents were and still are devout Catholics. Not only was attending Sunday Mass mandatory for my brothers and me, so were early-morning prayers—and I mean *early!* I'm sure it was actually a bit later than my memory is telling me now, but it seemed that prayers always happened at the crack of dawn.

Dad would barge into our bedrooms and drag his four bleary-eyed sons downstairs to say the rosary together. Most of the time I was still asleep as I began the first "Hail Mary," and I honestly wasn't aware of a word I'd uttered until I heard that all too welcome "Amen" escape my lips. Then, you see, I was able to return to bed until it was time to get ready for school.

Even though I would question Catholicism in my teenage years, I never lost faith that all of our lives, and the very universe itself, are guided by a force greater than ourselves—one that we cannot, perhaps, ever fully comprehend. Whether we call it God, the Divine, or simply Energy, it is a power that will enlarge our souls and enrich us if we have the courage to go through life with open minds and compliant hearts. It took me years to discover this immense truth, one I am still unraveling as I continue my living journey. However, I don't want to get too far ahead in my story. . . .

When I was six months old, my family moved from Metairie to the nearby town of Gretna. Our new house was big and had an amazing backyard, with plenty of space for a swing set, as well as room to play catch or tag.

It also had a big peanut-shaped swimming pool where we could retreat to escape the soupy-hot, sticky air of southeastern Louisiana summers.

I celebrated my first two birthdays in that sprawling, neatly mowed backyard with my entire family and some of the neighborhood kids my own age. Although I was too young to remember much about those parties or anything else from that time, my older brothers and parents have told me all about those early years. And since my dad was a home-movie fanatic, I've repeatedly watched countless hours of video chronicling our family life from 1980 onward.

On those earliest tapes, I can see my first and second birthday parties: the young, laughing guests; the giant cake; and me, tearing through piles of wrapping paper as gifts are placed in front of me. There's my mother smiling adoringly at me, and my father waving happily as he holds me in his arms. There are my two older brothers carrying me around the house, playing air guitar with me, and teaching me to walk and talk as though keeping me company was the greatest game ever invented.

It's strange to look at myself as I was during the first couple years of my life. Watching those flickering images is like glimpsing an alternate reality, one residing forever in a distant universe that I only occasionally retreat to in dreams. Nonetheless, in those videos I was a rambunctious, cute, sandy-haired kid with a mischievous smile; smooth, unblemished skin; and twinkling blue eyes that didn't have a care in the world. It was a lovely, idyllic time.

OTHER THAN IT BEING SAINT PATRICK'S DAY, there was nothing about the morning of March 17, 1982, that stood out or gave my family any reason to suspect that all of our lives were about to change forever. Of course, there never are any solid indicators that something profoundly good or overwhelmingly horrific is about to occur. Life just happens to us, deals us cards of fate, and it's our job to either endure the hand dealt or fold altogether. In my case, the life I was barely becoming aware of exploded, literally, in front of my young eyes.

I'm told that it was a particularly beautiful morning in southeastern Louisiana, sunny and mild without a hint of humidity. That Wednesday began like any other in our house: My parents rose early and had their morning prayers and breakfast done by 7:30 A.M. I was still in diapers, so naturally I stayed at home all day with my mom. My older brothers Johnny (who was nine at the time) and Scott (who was five) quickly dressed and shot out the door to catch the school bus. When Dad headed to work a few minutes later, Mom carried me outside with her so we could kiss him good-bye.

As my father pulled out of the driveway, my mother noticed that the grass in our yard was getting long. As a surprise for Dad, she decided to do something she'd never done before—mow the lawn herself. A short while later, she put me down in a fenced-in area of our patio that kept me away from our swimming pool, the most obvious threat of danger to a little boy just beginning to wander and investigate. I was an active, curious child; my mother has always told me that she loved that about me.

Mom set me down just a few feet away from where she was working in order to keep a close eye. She then went into the garage and filled the lawn mower with gasoline from a gas can my dad kept stored in the corner. She hauled the mower outside, started it up, and began the task at hand.

I was probably out of my mother's line of vision for less than ten seconds when she turned to push the lawn mower in the opposite direction, but that's all it took for me, a natural-born escape artist, to wander through the side door of the garage, probably in search of my favorite toy, a little plastic Flintstones wagon.

I'm not sure how it happened, either when I stepped into the garage or was pulling down one of my toys from a shelf, but somehow I knocked over the gas can my mom had used. Before I knew it, gasoline was pouring from the can and flooding across the concrete floor. An invisible cloud of fumes rose from the floor and within seconds had reached the pilot light of the water heater, which was standing in the far corner. A moment later, the garage exploded into a roaring inferno, and I was standing in the center of it. With the air around me blazing at nearly 2,000 degrees Fahrenheit, my skin instantly blistered and baked away, much of it to the bone.

It was a flash fire that lasted only an instant . . . but would stay with me for the rest of my life.

I DON'T REMEMBER THE EXPLOSION, THE FIRE, or the scream-ing afterward. But the piercing cry of her burning child sliced through the droning engine of the old lawn mower and directly into my mother's heart. She instantly bolted toward the garage and saw my limp, smoldering body sprawled across the now-blackened cement floor. I was dying and she knew it; her screams of terror penetrated the otherwise sedate neighborhood, prompting several neighbors to call for help. She was still screaming when it arrived.

Firefighters, sirens blaring, raced to us only minutes after the blast and immediately went to work, cutting the charred and melted clothes from my body. They lifted me into their arms and carried me out of the garage to the backyard, laid me down on the grass near the swimming pool, and tried to cool my boiling body and bring down my core temperature by pouring gallons of pool water over me. Ironically, the most "dangerous" part of our yard—the pool I had been fenced off from—became a major factor in my survival.

The one clear memory I have from that day is watching a fireman repeatedly dipping one of my mother's clay flowerpots into the pool and then carefully letting the water stream over me. I remember that the terra-cotta pot was emblazoned with a Native American design, and water flowed out of the drainage hole on the bottom as he rushed it toward me from the pool.

Paramedics arrived soon after, and Mom rode with me in the back of the ambulance so we could quickly get to Charity Hospital in New Orleans. Charity, which had one of the best trauma teams in the country and was the closest hospital to my home with a burn unit, was probably the only medical facility in the region with even the slightest chance of saving a child who had been virtually burned alive.

My father, who has written his own account of my accident (in his book *How Can YOU Play Drums?*), later told me how he first heard about what happened: a worried neighbor called him at work shortly after he'd arrived at the office, telling him that there had been a mishap at home and I'd been burned. Dad immediately got in his car and headed back to our house but wasn't overly concerned, thinking I'd suffered only a minor injury.

When my father arrived home, he was greeted by firefighters who filled him in on what had just happened. They tried to spare him the gory details, but he was able to find those out for himself when he saw the remnants of my tiny shirt laying on the garage floor beside the melted Snoopy sneakers the paramedics had cut from my feet and tossed aside.

Now fearing the worst, Dad had a neighbor drive him to Charity, where he found my mother sobbing inconsolably in the inner-city hospital's old waiting room. She was crying out that she wanted to hold her child, her baby, and fell into my father's arms when he came into the room. In stammers and starts, still unable to form complete sentences after the horror of what she'd witnessed, she tried to tell him what had happened.

My mother and father just held on to each other and prayed quietly until the emergency-room doctor brought them news of my condition. Suffice it to say, it wasn't good.

"Danny is in extremely critical condition," my parents were told. "He sustained third- and fourth-degree burns over nearly 80 percent of his body. His chances of surviving are very slim. Frankly, I don't know how he has lived this long. People burned this severely usually don't even survive the trip to the hospital."

The doctor gave them a list of things that could kill me in the coming hours, the most likely being infection or respiratory failure caused by lung damage from breathing in the burning, superheated air during the flash fire. I had literally eaten fire. All they could do, the doctor informed my parents, was to wait, and pray that I lived through the first critical 72 hours. And if I did manage to hang on to life, they had best make arrangements for treatment at another, more advanced medical facility because Charity Hospital couldn't properly care for anyone as chronically ill as I was going to be.

As grim a prognosis as it was, my parents didn't know that at that moment things were much worse than the doctor let on. I only discovered the truth about my condition very recently and quite by accident while I was traveling. By some odd chance of nature or design of God, I happened to bump into one of the doctors who had treated me soon after the fire.

"You died," he said bluntly, "and not just once. You died three times on the operating table, and I was able to bring you back three times after your heart stopped."

My life—that of the endearing young boy with an uncomplicated, normal existence mapped out before him like so many others who lived in our pleasant little neighborhood—ended on a pretty March afternoon in 1982 in an emergency operating room. There is no doubt: That boy died, and I was born. The third time I came back from the dead, I'd come to stay. I was holding on and wasn't letting go. Somehow I unconsciously knew that no matter how much fighting, suffering, and adversity my coming years might be filled with, it was the life I was destined to lead . . . the life I am leading now.

Of course, before I could start leading that new life, I had to survive the first night after being burned. At the time, that possibility seemed exceptionally remote.

It's hard for me to imagine what my parents were experiencing as those critical hours crept by. Whatever physical misery I was clearly suffering was equally as agonizing as the heartrending turmoil they endured, as they waited to hear if I would live or die. And if by some miracle I *did* survive, the prospect of all the obstacles that lay ahead of me undoubtedly gnawed at their hearts. At least I was sedated; their suffering, however, was as raw and palpable as it was inescapable.

I can never know exactly what my mother went through that day—her pain was so great that she has never once, even to this day, spoken to me about the accident. My father, on the other hand, has talked to me many times about the wild emotional ride that began for the Caro family the night of the gas explosion. As I mentioned earlier, Dad even managed to write his own account of how the fire affected us all, and many of the details I share now come by way of his tortured memories.

AFTER THE ER DOCTOR HAD THAT DIFFICULT TALK with my parents, a nurse arrived in the waiting room and whisked them into the corridor. She told them that I was out of surgery and the trauma team had done all they could for me at the moment—I was now to be transferred to intensive care in the burn unit. If my parents hurried, they could see me for just a few minutes before I was wheeled away.

Moments later, my mother and father were standing in a dimly lit hallway, looking down at a gurney holding the unconscious body of a little boy so badly mutilated that they didn't even recognize him.

That little boy was me.

But it's not surprising that my parents couldn't *tell* it was me. More than three-quarters of my skin had been burned off, my hair had been incinerated, and what was left of my face was obscured behind a plastic oxygen mask that was keeping me alive. Had the mask not been there, Mom and Dad would have seen that my lips and nose were gone. The doctor had also sliced open my arms and legs with a scalpel from my fingertips to my toes to allow body fluids to rise up and weep from the wounds rather than burst through the charred, parchment-thin remains of what had so recently been the flawlessly smooth flesh of a toddler.

My devastated parents grew physically faint at the sight of my ruined body and exposed tendons. They clung to each other, as much to remain standing as for the obvious emotional support. And then they could only watch silently as I was wheeled away toward the burn unit, leaving them alone in the hospital hallway to begin coping with the reality that their lives had been forever altered. They returned to the waiting room and kept vigil.

Arrangements were made for my brothers to be looked after as my parents realized that they wouldn't be going anywhere for a while. Most likely, they'd be staying at the hospital for the next 72 hours—hours that the doctor said would determine my fate.

Later that night, whatever hopes Mom and Dad may have been harboring deep inside that I wasn't in as bad a shape as I looked were dashed when they witnessed one of my first bandage changes.

My parents had kept asking to see me. Eventually, after dressing in sterile hospital scrubs and donning face masks and gloves, they were ushered into the burn unit, where they spent ten minutes beside my bed.

During this early bedside visit, a nurse unraveled the mummy-like bandages wrapped around my tiny body. My father was watching closely and saw, to his horror, that when she removed the bandages from my hands, my fingers came away in the gauze. They simply fell off. All ten fingers had been cooked to the bone, and those little bones were so charred and brittle that they now dropped off my hands, leaving me with two stumps at the end of either arm. My feet did not fare much better. As the bandages were cautiously removed from my left foot, so too did my toes peel away—they were now ruined, eaten by fire.

Dad was so distraught by the agony he believed I must be in that he begged the Lord to take me to heaven and end my pain. Yet, through her own tears, Mom prayed for me to be spared. She told Dad it didn't matter to her how maimed my body might be because I would always be loved. She wanted her baby to live; she craved to hold her Danny in her arms again.

From that moment on, my parents prayed in tandem. They both asked God for a miracle, and they got one.

As my parents wandered the desolate hallways between the waiting room and the burn unit through the night and into the next day, a steady stream of concerned relatives and friends arrived to show their support. Some prayed with them; others just sat with them silently; still others helped make arrangements for my brothers to get back and forth from home and school safely.

My father confided to a few around him that night how worried he was that Charity Hospital couldn't treat me once I was out of the ICU. He was panicked over money, having just quit a secure job at a large insurance firm to begin his own company. Dad was strapped financially at the time of my accident, and there was no way he could pay for a private hospital or the specialized long-term care and rehabilitation I was certainly going to require if I lived.

Out of the blue, his cousin Jimmy said, "John, I know a guy who's a Shriner. I think he said something to me once about the Shriners helping sick kids, especially ones who have been burned. Why don't I give him a call?"

Cousin Jimmy did just that, and within an hour, my dad was on a hospital pay phone with a Shriner named Joe Vita. Jimmy was right about the Shriners: they not only assisted with the care and treatment of sick kids, but they also had hospitals that specialized in pediatric burns.

Joe cut right to the chase, telling Dad that he had to make some quick decisions, and there wasn't a moment to lose. "Your boy is going to die in the bed he's in right now, John," Joe said. "Charity is a good hospital, but it's not remotely equipped to deal with his kind of injuries. But we *can* deal with them. We've been treating kids no one else could help since we built the first Shriners Hospital for Children in 1922. Trust me, we can save your son's life."

And then he made Dad an offer he couldn't refuse.

"Danny is going to need highly skilled, around-the-clock care for months, maybe years. The Shriners will do that for him; we'll take care of him for as long as he needs to be taken care of, and it won't cost you a dime. We'll pay for all his medical expenses. That's my offer to you, but you have to make up your mind. If your boy is going to live, he has to get to one of our hospitals right now. All you have to do is say the word, and we'll move him today. I don't know how we'll do it, but we *will* do it. You have my word on that."

Naturally, my dad accepted Joe's offer with gratitude. Our local chapter of the Shriners immediately got to work: they began checking with their hospitals to see which one had room for me, and they made arrangements with the doctors at Charity to transfer me. I was likely far too sick to travel, but I was also certain to die if I wasn't moved.

Late that afternoon, a bed had been found at the Shriners Hospital for Children in Boston, and a military medical jet had been booked to make the 1,300-mile flight. By eight o'clock that night—roughly 36 hours after the garage explosion—an ambulance rushed me to the military base in the New Orleans suburb of Belle Chasse, where a medevac jet was waiting on the tarmac. The seats had been stripped from the plane and replaced with medical equipment to make the aircraft a flying operating room. The medical team that had been keeping me alive at Charity Hospital also climbed on board with my parents to monitor my vital signs every second of the nearly four-hour flight.

We touched down at Logan International Airport sometime before midnight. My parents, still dressed for the hot Louisiana weather, shivered on the cold Massachusetts runway as I was loaded into yet another ambulance destined for the hospital. After they were ushered into a waiting police car, our family convoy headed into downtown Boston.

A team of doctors had already begun assessing me by the time my exhausted parents stumbled into the lobby of the hospital. There they were greeted by chief of staff Dr. John Remensnyder, who gave them the one thing they were desperately in need of—hope.

"I've examined Dan, and he looks bad. He's a very serious case. His chances are 50-50, but he has one thing going for him: he's at the finest pediatric burns hospital in the world. This is where miracles happen."

♦ ♦ ♦

Chapter Two

Out of the Ashes

They said I didn't cry when I began to move what was left of my body the next morning. I suppose I slipped in and out of consciousness in my sanitary-yet-toxic new world of glassed-in isolation, skin grafts, and operations.

The Shriners Hospital in Boston was my permanent home for four months after the fire, and in the years to follow, it became my home away from home. I had nearly 80 reconstructive surgeries before my 18th birthday, usually about four operations each year, and would spend a couple of weeks in the hospital for each procedure. Mom and I flew in and out of Boston so often that some of the pilots knew me by name. But when I woke up on that first morning, I was simply known as one of the most badly burned children the good folks at that hospital had ever seen.

If you've spent any time at all on a burn ward, you know that no matter how fine a facility or competent and caring a staff, it's not an easy place for a kid to be. The Shriners Hospital undoubtedly saved my life, but the hospital stay itself was incredibly difficult.

You see, I was in an environment populated by children who were in unimaginable pain and horribly disfigured. Kids around me were frequently near death or worse—and they were awake and aware of their agony. Many had become overwhelmed by despair and had given up on life.

As for me, I experienced moments of equally profound confusion, loneliness, and terror. But my stay at Shriners was also one of the greatest experiences of my life. Because I had so much time on my hands, I learned some life lessons as a child that most people don't learn until adulthood, if they are lucky to ever learn them at all.

In those sterile halls, I discovered that allowing yourself to be defined by how you look—or by what others say when they look at you—is the surest way to destroy your spirit. And yes, it was at Shriners that I discovered that we are spiritual beings who are just temporarily wrapped in flesh.

At the time, of course, I was just a little kid and didn't think about spirituality or life's important lessons. In fact, whatever I did discover about life back then I quickly forgot; it took me years of soul-searching to "remember" that I already understood an essential truth of the universe: what matters is who we are on the inside, not what we look like on the outside.

Even if it did take me another quarter century of living to rediscover that basic philosophy, the fact remains that the lessons I learned at Shiners were the most formative ones of my life. They shaped the person I would become and, in many ways, made me the person I am today.

ON THE MORNING OF MARCH 19, 1982—48 hours after the gasoline explosion—I wasn't having deep thoughts. Rather, I was a critically injured little boy teetering between life and death. I remember nothing of that morning; the combination of my young age, extreme trauma, and heavy doses of narcotic painkillers clouded my memories of my earliest days after the accident. Yet, remarkably, there are some moments and events from the very first week in Boston that I can recall with crystal clarity. Most of the gaps in my memory have been bridged through the recollections of others, such as my parents, whose first visits with me in that unfamiliar environment were as stressful as they were strange.

As one would assume, Mom and Dad had slept very little the night before. After leaving me at the hospital in the wee hours of the morning, they walked to the hotel room the Shriners had booked for them and collapsed into their bed. Before they knew it, the sun had risen and they were back at the hospital, with only caffeine and adrenaline keeping them on their feet.

They rode the elevator to the third floor, which was the one reserved for the most critically burned children. There were fewer than a dozen beds in the ward, each shrouded with heavy plastic tenting to stave off airborne infections. If a nurse hadn't led my mother and father to my bed and told them it was their son beneath the plastic, they never would have known who I was. Every inch of my body was wrapped in white bandages, and my face was doubly obscured by an oxygen mask. I was surrounded by beeping machines and tubes and wires running in every direction, feeding me liquid and drugs while keeping track of my racing heartbeat and unsteady blood pressure.

Eventually, my parents would be allowed to insert their gloved arms and hands through slits in the plastic curtains and gingerly stroke my bandaged body. Once again, doctors cautioned them that my fate was uncertain—if my lungs had been scorched, there wasn't much they'd be able to do for me.

Back at Charity Hospital in New Orleans, Mom and Dad had been told that the first 72 hours would determine if my lungs were okay and I had a shot at survival. Now they prayed for God to watch over me for another day, just 24 more hours. Once again, their prayers were answered.

Somehow I beat the odds and managed to live beyond that crucial 72-hour threshold, and that's when the struggle of being a survivor began. My parents found out how complex that struggle was going to be when they first saw me with no bandages at all. They'd been warned that it would be a hideous shock for them, and the warning was well founded.

As my face appeared from beneath the bandages, Mom and Dad saw that most of it was gone: I had no nose, lips, or eyelids; and my ears were melted. Almost all of my hair had vanished, and the roots were obliterated as well. They already knew that my fingers had come away with that first bandage removal, as had the toes on my left foot. As far as they could see, the only place I hadn't been burned was my groin and buttocks—it turns out that these areas had been protected from the fire by a soggy diaper.

In that first full glimpse of my injuries, I'm sure I didn't even appear human to my mother and father, much less look like their child.

BECAUSE SO MUCH OF MY SKIN had been burned away, one of the first things the doctors had to do was graft new skin onto the raw muscle, meat, and tendon left exposed. Fortunately, those doctors would be able to use skin from the roughly 20 percent of my body that hadn't been burned to graft onto the parts where the skin had come off entirely. That was a blessing, because by using the few patches of good skin I had on my stomach, the back of my head, and the diaper-protected area, they'd avoid the problems of tissue rejection that occur when an organ (and skin is the body's largest organ) from one person is transplanted in another.

But until I was strong enough to donate my own skin, the surgeons had to use donor skin from a "skin bank." Donor skin was frequently used even after I was strong enough to donate my own, since once the small patches of transplantable skin I had were removed for grafting, it took several weeks for them to regrow enough to harvest again. This meant I was always in danger of organ rejection, which put my already-weakened immune system under constant attack. My exposed wounds and new skin were also an open invitation to bacteria, and I'd be plagued by more staphylococcal infections than I could count.

If the director of a horror movie ever asked me for advice on how to terrify an audience, my answer would be: "Film a kid getting prepped for a skin graft." The seemingly endless cycle of grafts I endured began within a few days of my arrival in Boston. The doctors decided I would have two of them a week and, as young as I was, I knew exactly when those treatments were about to begin. A team of doctors and nurses, or sometimes just the nurses, would arrive at my bed with a particularly sympathetic look in their eyes that silently said, "Sorry, Danny . . . this is going to hurt us more than it's going to hurt you." That's when the process known as debridement would begin.

Debridement simply means the removal of dead tissue—and after my accident, I was covered in dead skin that had to be removed before the new skin could be grafted on. There were several methods of debridement, and I found each one to be more horrible than the last, especially since for some reason I was never allowed to have painkillers or sedatives for any of the procedures.

Sometimes the nurses would forcibly hold down my wildly squirming body while forceps were used to grab and peel away large flakes of dead skin embedded in my raw flesh, or while a doctor used a scalpel to cut away decaying tissue. But the "tub method" was definitely the most terrifying: I'd be lowered into a stainless-steel whirlpool and held fast by several nurses while one of their colleagues used a wire brush that looked like an enormous Brillo Pad to sweep away whatever dead bits of skin still stubbornly clung to my battered little body.

I remember the contrast between the nurses' vice-like grips and their soothing voices as I thrashed about in vain, fighting desperately to escape their clutches and avoid the torturous treatment. All the while, they'd promise me it would be over soon, until they'd finally say in singsong unison, "There now, Danny, it's all done . . . all done." Those two words became a kind of hospital mantra for me. Whenever I spied a group of nurses approaching my bed with that sympathetic look in their eyes, I'd throw my bandaged arms up in protest and repeatedly declare in my most insistent voice that we were "All done! All done!"

My father told me that he still feels sick to his stomach whenever he recalls the times he was asked to help hold me during a debridement session. "It nearly killed me to watch you go through that," he says today. "Your screams must have echoed across the entire hospital. Half of Boston heard your suffering."

Yet as agonizing as the whole process was, it's the *anticipation* of the pain I remember, not the pain itself. In fact, I can't recall being in pain before, during, or after my stay in the hospital. With the exception of my first few days in the ICU, I wasn't put on a morphine drip and was rarely given opiates.

Even when I was older and hooked up to self-administering morphine drips after surgery, I never once pushed the button to give myself a shot—there was no need. I guess the logical explanation is that the pain receptors in my nerve endings were destroyed when the fire burned away most of my skin. But I don't think that's it because I still don't feel pain, even in places where I wasn't burned. When I pulled my arm out of my shoulder socket not too long ago, all I experienced was some mild discomfort. Even when I had my wisdom teeth taken out, I stunned the dentist by telling him to just give me a mild anesthetic and start drilling.

In my mind, the reason I didn't feel physical pain as a kid and don't feel it now is that there was something greater at work. Honestly, I believe that my parents' many bedside prayers asking for my pain to end did the trick. To this day, I think that the thoughts and wishes we put out into the universe—be they positive or negative— come back to us and manifest themselves in our lives. That's why I always try to send out the most positive energy in my thoughts and deeds. I've seen the power of what many call "positive thinking," and I both believe in it and respect it immensely.

The power of the loving energy my parents surrounded me with in Boston made all the difference in my recovery. For the first two weeks after the accident, they both spent every day in the hospital with me. But the world didn't stop because I'd been hurt, so Dad had to fly back to Louisiana to look after my brothers and take care of his fledgling insurance company.

My father would come back to see me for weekend visits, but my mother stayed by my side. With the exception of a short trip or two back home, she was with me in Boston for the entire four months. Luckily, Mom and Dad made some friends who lived just outside of town, and they let Mom stay at their house and even lent her a car to make it easier to travel to and from the hospital.

AFTER MY MIRACULOUS FEAT OF SURVIVING the first 72 hours after the accident, I showed little signs of improvement for the next six weeks. Each day my mother would sit at my bedside from early morning until visiting hours were over. She'd stare at my listless body, lying as still as death inside the plastic tent, but she'd keep talking to me as though I could hear every word she uttered.

Mom would tell me over and over that she loved me; fill me in on the news from home, including what my big brothers were doing at school; and encourage me to keep fighting because the sooner I got better, the sooner I could be outside playing with the other kids again. She would stroke my face over my bandages, sing lullabies, and read my favorite children's stories to me. Although I don't recall much of her bedside vigil, I credit it with keeping me going all those weeks.

Nevertheless, for the better part of two months it seemed to both my family and the hospital staff that even if I beat the odds and stayed alive, I might never again be the irrepressibly energetic and mischievous little boy I'd been before. But after my father brought me a special treat one weekend, my spirits and my prospects for a full recovery suddenly soared. I'm not saying that Rocky Balboa saved my life, but he definitely made me want to get out of bed and fight to get better.

For as long as I can remember, *Rocky II*, starring Sylvester Stallone as the wannabe comeback champ, has been my favorite movie. My brothers loved it, too, and played it over and over again on the VCR. I'm sure I'd seen the movie a dozen times before I began speaking, and I was throwing jabs and uppercuts before I took my first step. For some reason, it resonated with me in every way: the simple story of the underdog never giving up on a dream; the unrelenting urge to be the best you can be despite all odds; the craggy trainer, Mickey, who never cut Rocky any slack; the goose-bump-raising scene where a couple hundred schoolchildren join Rocky as he runs up the steps of the Philadelphia Museum of Art; and most of all, the rousing musical score by Bill Conti that still makes me want to climb into the ring whenever I hear it.

Knowing my passion for this movie, Dad brought an audio recording of it with him during one of his visits. I don't know what he expected, but as soon as he turned on the cassette player and I heard the theme song crackling out of the tiny speaker, my entire near-comatose body started to shake and twitch. Within minutes, my bandaged foot was tapping the air along with the beat of the music—and I was struggling to sit up in bed, crawl out of my tent, and start running across the floor of the burn ward.

My parents were overjoyed by my reaction to the tape. They began to see that behind the plastic and beneath the bandages, the high-spirited little Danny they loved was alive and kicking. They'd just witnessed me taking my first tentative steps on the very long road of recovery. I think they realized that, like the character of Rocky whom I admired so much, I wasn't going to let anyone throw in the towel or stop me from going the entire 15 rounds.

Two weeks later, Dad returned to Boston with a pair of children's boxing gloves packed in his luggage. During those two weeks, I'd rejected some of my newly grafted skin and developed a staph infection with an accompanying fever. By the time my father arrived on the ward with my new boxing gloves, however, I'd improved enough so that the surgeon let him carefully slip the gloves over my bandaged wrists. As soon as Dad laced them up, I began taking friendly jabs at the doctors and nurses.

About two months after that first "boxing match" with the hospital staff in Boston, I was well enough to go home to Louisiana.

IT WAS MID-JULY, FOUR MONTHS AFTER THE ACCIDENT. While I was now technically an outpatient, I still flew back to Shriners every two or three months for reconstructive surgery on my face, head, feet, hands, and just about any other body part you can name. So much of my childhood was spent in that hospital that I feel I never really left.

But as I mentioned earlier, I learned many life lessons in Boston. The first was that if you're going to pick a role model to fashion yourself after, you could do a lot worse than Rocky Balboa. Even though a lot of people roll their eyes at me when I say how much I identify with that character, I wouldn't be anywhere in life if I hadn't started emulating the underdog's never-say-die fighting spirit when I wasn't yet three years old, trapped beneath a plastic tent, wrapped head to toe in bandages. Rocky helped make me a fighter—and if I hadn't learned to fight, I'd be dead.

I had to fight to get through the dozens upon dozens of reconstructive surgeries I was to endure. For most people, a change in season means a change in the weather; for me it meant another 1,300-mile trip to have a part of my body rebuilt.

As you might imagine, the main reason I had so many operations was because my injuries were so severe. But you might not realize that another reason was that I was so young and still growing, which meant that the doctors had to redo their work as my bones got longer. Let me tell you, what they did was really amazing, cutting-edge stuff. Just for starters, they rebuilt my nose using part of my ribs, built my cheeks using a new type of synthetic material, used skin from the back of my head to design new eyelids, and created a thumb on my left hand where none existed.

Secretly, I suspect that those surgeons thought of me as their personal version of Steve Austin, the "bionic man" from the TV show *The Six Million Dollar Man.* I'm not sure if you remember it, but Colonel Steve Austin (portrayed by Lee Majors) was an astronaut who was horribly injured when his experimental aircraft crashed during a test flight. When he was pulled from the fiery wreckage, it was discovered that he'd lost both legs and an arm, and was blind in one eye. Like me, Austin landed in a hospital where miracles happen. When things looked bleakest for him, a scientist uttered these famous fictional words to the colonel's medical team: "Gentlemen, we can rebuild him . . . better than he was before."

I'd like to think the doctors made *me* better than I was before. I'm certain they made me stronger and faster than I would've been without their creative genius. In fact, I became one of the fastest kids in the neighborhood after one particular surgery, which moved a tendon on my twisted left foot in an effort to pull the bone to the right. Within a couple of days of that operation, I was running wild. I had a huge boot on my leg (the kind you see on people who have had skiing accidents), and I used the momentum of the boot to propel me forward. I ran like I had wings on my feet—like little Forrest Gump and his braced legs. When the boot came off, I could run even faster . . . and once I started running, I never wanted to stop.

Having all that energy made returning to the confines of the burn ward all the more restrictive during my stays there. As I grew older and stronger, I regularly struck out to explore the greater universe of the hospital. I quickly discovered where the gurneys were stored and began organizing races with other young burn patients. Sometimes we'd race each other by pushing our gurneys solo; other times we'd make it more like chariot races, with one kid pushing and another riding atop the gurney's mattress.

We liked to race along the underground corridor that connected Shriners Hospital with Massachusetts General Hospital across the street. The long tunnel had a natural dip in it, which was great for gathering speed and irresistible to fun-loving kids with a set of wheels. Unfortunately, not everyone appreciated our enthusiasm. After we accidentally clipped some doctors with a speeding gurney—and sent one of my competitors to surgery to have a dozen stitches closed up after a nasty pileup—the famous Shriners Gurney Races were shut down.

But I continued to explore the hospital. Sometimes I'd do so by myself, but I often went with a local volunteer who visited the burn ward twice a week. I knew him simply as "Shriner Bob," and what I remember most about him is that he was superfriendly to every patient he met. Shriner Bob would lead a group of us youngsters on tours of every floor of the hospital, even those restricted to medical staff, where we on the ward were forbidden to go.

It was always an incredible adventure when Bob showed up and told us to prepare ourselves for an expedition. The group of us would trek across the entire length of the underground passageway, the former racetrack for our gurneys, to the other side into Mass General. There, Shriner Bob would take us into the gift shop to buy comic books, small toys, and sweets before returning us safely to the burn ward.

Those trips may not seem like much, but for a kid whose world was confined to the space between the metal rails of a hospital bed, crossing a tunnel and coming out through the other side was like getting in a spaceship and leaving the solar system. Bob showed me that people were capable of random acts of kindness, and that there was a great unknown universe waiting for me once I got better and could leave the hospital.

As I got older, my horizons would expand even further when a friend took me on a day trip to go whale watching on the New England coastline, or when someone who heard about my love of basketball invited me to a Boston Celtics game. But those early trips through the tunnel with Shriner Bob stand out in my mind.

It was during my exploration of the hospital that I began to wrestle with deep philosophical issues five-year-olds have no business thinking about. Sometimes I'd pass through different wards in the hospital and see kids curled up in their beds with their heads buried beneath their blankets. They'd just lie there for weeks, never looking beyond the foot of their beds or acknowledging that there were other children who were suffering just as much as they were on either side of them. To be sure, they were in some level of pain, but for the most part their afflictions were being treated. I could see that what was trapping them in their beds was not physical pain but fear. They couldn't accept whatever injury had happened to them and didn't know how to cope with the personal battles ahead. Instead, they retreated beneath their blankets.

Being intimately acquainted with the challenges a young burn victim faces, I was empathetic when I saw these kids. But as I grew older, I'd see the same attitude everywhere I looked in the world, and not just in the hospital. I realized that whether we are 4 or 44, we are responsible for making choices about how we deal with difficulties—we can face them head-on, or we can hide.

I made a choice at a very young age to confront the world and not hide away just because I was afraid of something. It was perhaps a more practical decision than a courageous one; I mean, *look* at me! Even back then, I knew I'd never be able to hide what happened to me or conceal the way I looked. Years later I saw a movie—which went on to become one of my all-time favorites—called *The Shawshank Redemption,* in which the lead character says that the course of everyone's life is determined by one simple choice: get busy living, or get busy dying.

At five years old, I chose to get busy living.

OTHER LESSONS WOULD PRESENT THEMSELVES to me at Shriners Hospital during my return visits. As I said, I learned early on the folly of viewing yourself based on how others see you. My first inkling of that truth came when I noticed the way parents of other, less severely burned patients looked at me.

You may find it hard to believe that discrimination based on physical appearance would exist on a burn ward, but believe me, it does. As early as age four, I remember noticing the looks and hearing the whispers when I'd walk by the bed of a new arrival on the ward. "Thank God—at least our child doesn't look like that!" one mother said once. Another time, a family literally backed up against a wall when I wandered past them. Most of the time I just heard gasps of horror as I approached, or snickering and "Tsk-tsk" behind my back. These reactions stung.

Ever since I'd been discharged, my parents had kept me close to home for the most part. Home was safe: Mom and Dad protected me from the judgmental eyes of the public, and my brothers—with the exception of a "no roughhousing" policy—treated me as they always had. Now I found myself being confronted by prejudice in the very place one would expect the most sympathy and understanding.

Those upsetting reactions didn't happen often, because my mother was with me most of the time. Mom protected me like a mother bear and was fierce with people who treated me unfairly or with disrespect. Yet the cruel looks and cutting remarks on those few occasions when I was alone in the hospital troubled and confused me. I couldn't understand it—every kid on the ward was scarred or disfigured in some way, so weren't we all the same? What was it about the way *I* looked that made grown-ups back away in fear or even say mean and hurtful things?

At first I was taken aback by their attitude and stewed about it during the many long days I spent alone in the germ-free isolation room after surgery. Somehow, and I'm still not sure how, my young mind was open and versatile enough to believe that there was nothing wrong with me; if there *was* something wrong, it was with the adults who'd treated me poorly.

I studied my reflection in the mirror—and finding a mirror on a burn ward is not an easy task—the way an artist would study his subject. The longer I looked at my face, the more pleased I became with it. I appreciated the way I looked and the fact that I had, for starters, two holes in the center of my face instead of a nose. I was unique! Eventually, I decided that it didn't matter what strangers thought of me. Everyone who knew me loved me, and I was determined to love myself, too. To hell with what other people thought!

Of course, I was just a kid and hadn't experienced the harsh reality of life yet. That would come a little later, when I entered the dog-eat-dog world of kindergarten.

♦ ♦ ♦

Chapter Three

A New Thumb, and New Challenges

When I first arrived home from my initial four-month stay at the hospital, my family had to adjust to having a delicate child in their midst. Before the accident I'd been a bouncy, resilient kid who clamored to be in the thick of things. Now things were vastly different. Dad and Mom put my two big brothers on high alert: they could play with me but had to be careful not to knock me over, nor could they haul me around the house as they often did before the fire. I was still a very sick, severely injured little boy who was extremely fragile.

At first, my family had to do everything for me. Mom, quite literally, became a nurse to me. She changed my bandages several times each day, spoon-fed me, helped me go to the bathroom, and was my main link to the world around me.

Still, I was an energetic youngster and curious about the world. The fire hadn't burned away my desire to be part of everything that was going on in my midst, and I was included in all the family activities (even if everyone had to be supervigilant about my safety and keep an extracareful eye out if I wandered off somewhere in the house). Sure, I had weekly sessions with a physiotherapist and had a gazillion doctor and hospital visits, but thanks to my parents' and brothers' total acceptance of me as an equal member of the family, I felt like a normal kid during those first couple of years back home.

Of course, I was far from normal.

By the age of two or three, most children have mastered the simple everyday tasks people perform a hundred times a day without thinking about them. Picking up a fork, combing one's hair, pulling on a pair of pants, and the like are automatically done without a second thought. But for me, those everyday tasks became gargantuan undertakings. At least they were at first, when I was trying to do things the way everyone else did them, which was impossible.

Take using cutlery, for example. I must have tried to pick up a spoon to dig into a bowl of pudding a thousand times before it became obvious that without fingers, I wasn't going to eat like everyone else did. One of my physiotherapists tried to remedy that situation by fastening a strap onto my wrists and sticking a fork under the right wrist strap and a knife under the left one. It was a total disaster. Either the utensils dropped to the floor or the chinaware did.

I was born with a deeply rooted independent streak, so not being able to do things for myself was very troubling. I kept trying to do everything on my own by copying what everyone else did, and I kept failing. Finally, I decided that if I couldn't do things the way "normal" people did, then the normal rules didn't apply to me. This was an incredibly important lesson for me to learn at an early age, and extremely liberating!

I glanced at the ends of my arms and told myself that if I didn't have fingers, there was no point in acting like I did. Instead, I'd start working with what I had—I'd simply use the ends of both of my arms to pick up my fork and bring food to my mouth. Success! At that moment, I could feed myself, and my entire future was suddenly changed. I would no longer be dependent on either the kindness of strangers or the goodness of my family. I would now take care of myself.

Next, I realized that if I could manipulate a fork with my two arms, then why couldn't I do the same with a pen? Soon I was doodling and eventually writing by gripping a pen between both arms. Then I discovered that by using my mouth and wrists together, I could button my shirt. Before long I'd learned how to do just about every daily task all by myself: I could pull on my pajamas, slip into a T-shirt, and zip up a zipper. I could also toss a Frisbee and swing a baseball bat. I could even use a bow and arrow on family camping trips.

I may not have looked particularly graceful doing most things, such as using my mouth to yank a button through a buttonhole, but I didn't care what I looked like. What mattered was that I was doing almost everything on my own and in my own way . . . except tying my shoelaces. No matter how hard I tried, I couldn't grasp those narrow laces and pull them into a knot. While shoelaces were a source of constant frustration for me, I was proud that I'd accomplished so much and mastered so many other everyday challenges.

Then I turned five. That's when the doctors told me that they thought they could successfully build a "thumb" on my left hand. As I've already mentioned, I've had scores of reconstructive surgeries since the fire, but the series of operations in which my thumb was constructed stands out most clearly in my mind because it changed my life in so many wonderful ways, allowing me to accomplish more than anyone ever dreamed possible.

Believe it or not, I hated the change at first. It had taken nearly three years after returning from my initial stint in Boston to become independent performing most daily tasks. But after my new thumb, I had to learn to do everything all over again! It was like being sent back a few grades in school and told that everything you'd learned up to then was all a lie! *Start over, kid! Do it again!*

Actually, the fact that they figured out how to build me a thumb from my own flesh and bone (and a little bit of steel wire for good measure) was pretty amazing. The procedure was complex and involved separating my first metacarpal from the rest of the bones in my left hand, elongating it with wires, and then slowly "twisting" the bone over time. I had at least five separate thumb surgeries, and after each one, I had to wear a metal cage over my hand. The doctors at Shriners called it a "hay raker" because it looked like the rake farmers used during harvest to collect (you guessed it) hay. The doctors also harvested my own skin to graft the new thumb, which eventually allowed me to grip and hold things quite firmly.

As I said, though, I had to relearn everything I'd already accomplished and was pretty upset about my new digit at first. It seemed as though I'd gone through a ton of work up to that point for nothing. My doctors sent me to physical therapy to learn how to use the thumb, but I refused to cooperate at first. I had been getting along fine without one and hoped that if I just ignored it, it might go away. But it *didn't* go away—and as time went by and I got used to that thumb, my whole world opened up.

IT WAS DURING THE NEW STRUGGLE to master my thumb that I first began to notice God in my life. Of course, just like when I was in the hospital and intuitively sensed that I was a spiritual being, I wasn't actually thinking about God specifically. What happened after I started using my thumb is that I caught a glimpse of the possibilities life held in store for me—or for any of us—when fear is put aside and we open ourselves up to the universe. I became aware of the soul's desire to be inspired and to achieve a dream. In short, I began to *realize* God without *understanding* it. For me, "God" was the force pushing me from within to get the job done and move my heart and mind forward. I developed a belief that I could run headlong and headstrong toward any challenge with assurance and confidence. It gave me an immense feeling of freedom.

Until I looked down at my shoes.

Tying your shoes is harder than you think. Although little kids usually spend weeks learning how to do it, they then have it down pat for the rest of their lives and never give it another thought. My experience, as you can imagine, was a little different. Even with my new thumb, the task of tying my shoes was more difficult and more frustrating than anything I'd had to endure up until that point.

Ironically, while my new thumb was opening up a galaxy of possibilities for me, the fact that I couldn't tie my shoes haunted me like a demon. My inability to perform this task created such a deep sense of personal failure in me that I secretly began to view it as a kind of character flaw.

My parents thought they'd addressed the problem when they brought home loafers, slip-ons, and Velcro-closing running shoes for me. But those shortcuts just intensified my embarrassment; I was ashamed to be the only one in the neighborhood wearing Velcro sneakers. Still, I wasn't about to let my shoelaces mock the fresh sense of possibility my new thumb had given me. Instead of admitting defeat, I promised myself that no matter how long it took or how difficult it was, I'd practice tying my shoes every day of my life until I succeeded. At five years old, I made tying my shoelaces my mission in life.

In the meantime, I was getting older, and some of the greatest challenges of my life were about to begin.

MY TWO OLDER BROTHERS WERE ENROLLED at the local Christian school in our area, and my parents assumed that I'd follow in their footsteps. But when Mom and Dad talked to the administration, they were told it was impossible—the school board didn't think the facility could accommodate my "special needs." Out of ignorance, the board assumed that because I looked different from other kids,

I must have some kind of learning disability or need extraordinary help.

My parents objected to this decision, and the Shriners even offered to send one of their ambassadors to the school to explain that I had no special requirements. Yet none of this made any difference. The board's actions were stupid and mean and, I have to say, not very "Christian." It was the first case of "official" discrimination I'd encountered because of the way I looked. My parents were so furious that they pulled one of my brothers out of that school in protest.

Mom and Dad ended up enrolling me in Terrytown Academy, a private school that accepted me with open arms. A Shriner ambassador had visited the facility before the school year and chatted with the staff about me, explaining that although my injuries made me appear different, I was a normal, happy kid who didn't need or want any unique attention or assistance. He even passed around photographs of me to the teachers and administrators to ensure that no one would react in shock when meeting me in person. Everyone at Terrytown was well prepared for my arrival in kindergarten that September . . . everyone except my fellow students, that is, who did their best to make my life a living hell.

It was bad right from the start. At first the teachers kept watch to make sure the other kids were on their best behavior, but I could feel my classmates' eyes on me when my back was turned. The energy they silently projected my way was so negative I felt it would suffocate me. It was the first time I sensed hatred, and after that first day at school, the idea of returning made me cringe. I didn't tell my parents what was going on—I was embarrassed by how the kids felt about me, and I didn't want Mom and Dad to see my shame. Instead, I bottled everything up inside and didn't say a word about it to anybody.

On the second day of school, I dreaded getting out of bed and putting on my uniform. When my brothers and I met in our parents' room for morning prayers, I prayed that something would happen to Terrytown Academy so I wouldn't have to go. Alas, those negative prayers weren't answered. So after breakfast I reluctantly climbed in the passenger seat of the family minivan, buckled up my seat belt, and sat back powerlessly as my mother drove the two miles to Terrytown.

On the third day, I was so upset that I refused to get out of the van when my mother parked in the cul-de-sac in front of the big brick schoolhouse. Mom, still not understanding my hesitation, walked me to the kindergarten classroom and left me with the teacher, Mrs. Wingfield, who escorted me inside.

Mrs. Wingfield was your stereotypical schoolmarm, probably 60 or 65 years old and very prim and proper. Her hair was completely gray and wrapped so tightly in a bun on the top of her head that I was certain it was going to pull her face off. As she led me to my seat, the faces of the other children twisted into masks of contempt and horror. Every fiber of my being screamed for me to run away as fast as possible, so that's exactly what I tried to do. But Mrs. Wingfield held on to me and, in a very calm and gentle voice, asked what was troubling me.

How does a five-year-old explain an anxiety attack or the feeling of absolute terror? I answered the only way I knew how—by kicking her in the shins as hard as I could.

I kicked and punched until she finally let go of me, and I made a mad dash for the door. I ran down the hallway as fast as my feet would carry me, until I burst through the doors and was safely outside. In the distance, I saw our white minivan pulling away from the school property and screamed out at the top of my lungs, "Mom!" The van came to an abrupt halt, and my mother's comforting arms were soon around me. But even then I couldn't tell her how horribly uncomfortable I was in school . . . so I found myself back in the classroom, silently suffering in a sea of youthful hostility.

But whatever discomfort I experienced in class was nothing compared to the torture I was subjected to in the school yard during recess. Whenever I walked onto the playground, I'd find myself encircled by dozens of taunting kids who hurled razor-sharp insults at me with the kind of unfiltered cruelty that comes naturally to some children.

"Look at the ugly monster!" they'd shout.

"Hey, Frankenstein!"

"Freak . . . freak . . . freak! Go back where you came from, burn boy! We don't want you here!"

When I tried to walk away, the kids walked backward, keeping pace with me and holding me in the center of their wicked little circle. If I rushed at them, they'd scatter, shouting over their shoulders at each other as they ran: "Look out! The monster is trying to catch you. Run!"

The same nightmare repeated itself day after day. When my mother picked me up in the afternoons and asked how school was, I'd just shrug my shoulders and mumble that it was okay. Once we were home, I'd retreat to my room and spend hours unsuccessfully trying to tie my shoes, pulling at my laces until my new thumb was rubbed raw, or until Mom called me to come downstairs for supper.

After a week or so, I started avoiding the school yard altogether. As soon as the bell rang for recess, I'd make a beeline for the fence on the far side of the property, slip through an opening in the metal, and begin walking the perimeter of Terrytown Academy.

Circling the school property during recess, I began a daily ritual of carefully observing the different groups of children as they formed together in cliques to play games or share gossip. They all looked so harmless from my safe, distant, and anonymous vantage point. I wondered how the sweet faces of the little girls happily skipping in and out of a blur of swinging jump rope could have become so evil when they'd cornered me just a week before. I stopped and listened to them singing:

> *Girl Guide, Girl Guide, dressed in yellow,*
> *This is the way I treat my fellow:*
> *Hug him, kiss him, kick him in the pants,*
> *That is the way to find romance . . .*

Not far from the skipping girls, a dozen boys from my kindergarten class were laughing together and slapping one another on the back as they horsed around and traded baseball cards. Their group looked so friendly and inviting, but when I'd tried to join them several days earlier, they'd turned on me viciously and mocked me until my eyes burned with tears.

Day in and day out, I'd study the various groups in the school yard, and I began to see a definite social structure. Obviously, the kids who associated within each group were linked by age and grade level, but within each grade I noticed a pecking order determined by popularity, looks, and charisma. And at the top of the kindergarten pecking order was a boy named Kieran.

Kieran was the tallest boy in our grade, with a handsome face and a wide smile that instantly put the other kids at ease. He was by far the most athletic boy as well, so physically graceful that he made tossing a football across the length of the yard or making an impossible softball catch seem effortless. To top things off, he was fast—faster than many boys twice his age.

But what I found most intriguing about Kieran was that he was a natural leader. Other kids clamored around him, looking to him to decide what the game of the day would be, and he'd organize them quickly into teams without rancor or argument. He never seemed bossy or used his popularity to lord over others—he just seemed like a really nice, fun kid to be around. And while he never stepped in to stop the other kids from picking on me, I don't ever recall him joining in on the many occasions the kindergarten mob turned on me.

Often I'd look at the kids playing around Kieran and wonder what it would be like to join them, but I knew what would happen if I tried. I was lonely, but I preferred solitude to ridicule. So I watched from afar and continued to study my schoolmate adversaries. If a teacher approached me and asked why I didn't join the others at play, I'd whisper something about preferring to walk by myself and hustle away until the bell rang. At home

I remained silent about my emotional turmoil, continuing to conceal my growing psychological anguish. It was unbearable, and I was miserable. There is little doubt in my mind that at the age of five I was heading for an emotional breakdown.

And that's when I first felt myself open completely to the universe and somehow tap into a power that was beyond myself, beyond anything that my limited experience had prepared me for.

THE DAY STARTED LIKE EVERY OTHER: I arrived in class, was greeted by muttered jeers and derision as I walked to my desk, and then sat sullenly until the recess bell rang and I could flee from the school yard and walk the perimeter in peace. But on that particular day, I felt a shift—not only in my mood, but also in the very way the energy of the world seemed to be flowing around me. Everything was different. My senses became sharper, and I felt stronger than I'd ever felt before.

Again, I don't know if it was God giving me the gift of self-awareness or what, but on that particular morning I had a revelation. I received a flash of inspiration that convinced me I had the power to change the world around me, including the things that were making me miserable. The feeling grew so strong in me that I came to a sudden, dead stop in the middle of my perimeter walk and turned toward the playground.

As usual, the boys were gathering around Kieran, who was organizing a game of tag. He had them huddled into a circle to decide who was going to be "it." As I watched them, I felt a sudden push, as if someone had shoved me forward. Then I felt it again. I took a step and caught myself. I remember turning around for a split second to see who'd done the pushing, but there was no one there. As I turned my attention back to the boys in the huddle, I was suddenly consumed by a new feeling of contentment, and I heard these words in my head: *Whatever it takes, you will make a friend today. Now go!*

I felt invincible.

Without another moment's thought, my feet began to move, and I found myself running at full tilt toward the little knot of boys huddled around Kieran. When they saw me coming, they immediately screamed, "Look out, he's coming! The monster is coming! Run for your life!"

The huddle of boys scattered, but I had set my sights on my target. I was going after Kieran, and I chased him all over the playground. He was running as fast as I'd seen him run before, but I kept gaining on him. I felt another surge of energy, another push from beyond, and—wham! The next thing I knew, I had the fastest and most popular boy in kindergarten in a full tackle. We skidded along the ground and began to wrestle. He fought hard, but I was stronger and finally pinned him down.

A crowd had gathered around us by this time, and every one of the kids stood there with their mouths open. The silence was deafening. I stood up and then helped Kieran up, too, and we stared at each other for a moment or two. Then he reached out to me, clasped my wrist with his hand, and introduced himself. Even though the chasing and wrestling had been a violent burst on my part, it put a stop to the ticking time bomb inside me. My anger and emotional misery fizzled away at that moment. I felt only peace and joy as Kieran turned to the other boys and girls around us and said that I was now his friend.

A surge of raw energy shot through me. Again, I don't know if it was God taking a spin through my soul for a moment or what, but I know I'd never experienced anything like it before. The surge was a little bit scary to me when it happened, but only because it was so unfamiliar—as unfamiliar as suddenly being accepted. I felt like a door had opened inside of me. I realized that I'd been my own worst enemy, that I'd allowed myself to be consumed by fear, and others had picked up on that. When I tackled Kieran, I'd taken on my own fear, and I emerged victorious.

Kieran was now my friend, and because he was so popular, the other kids followed his lead. I'm not saying that everything about my "differences" faded away like magic, but this acceptance allowed me the ability to stop erecting my own roadblocks (which I hadn't even realized I'd been building). From that day on, school was no longer a burden to be dreaded. I began to grow, both physically and academically.

I began to take part in class discussions and work in study groups without feeling like a complete outcast. I even started to play games with the other kids—real games of basketball, soccer, kickball, baseball, and football. I knew I'd finally discovered that elusive thing that every other kid takes for granted: childhood. Now I had a shot at a relatively normal one, with genuine friends I could bring home and play with.

Over the next couple of years, I made more and more friends. At the end of each school year, I also routinely saw my name on the dean's list—by the fourth grade, my grades were among the highest in the academy.

As I slowly grew used to my new thumb, I found that I could do more and more things that otherwise would have been impossible. Although I still couldn't tie my shoelaces, I no longer considered this to be a failure; it was just a challenge that I knew I'd conquer one day. I loved my new life, my newfound sense of being a boy. I'd lost so much by giving in to my own insecurities and fears, and now I'd taken it back.

I reclaimed my life, and I was determined to excel.

♦ ♦ ♦

Chapter Four

Making Miracles

I was seven years old in the fall of 1986, and that's when my parents heard rumors circulating around their church about miraculous cures happening in Europe. Parishioners in the congregation were talking about the wonders that were supposedly occurring in a remote village in what was then Yugoslavia (now Bosnia and Herzegovina) called Medjugorje. Supernatural visitations by the Virgin Mary were said to have begun in 1981, just two years after I was born. Over the course of the next five years, the little town had been transformed from an obscure Balkan backwater to a world-famous apparition site and pilgrimage destination.

The claim was that Mary had selected a small group of children in Medjugorje to appear before and share her messages from heaven, as she'd reportedly done on many occasions with other children around the world since the death of her son, Jesus Christ. Mary repeatedly appeared as a vision to these Yugoslavian boys and girls, speaking only to them even though there were often others, including grown-ups, present. The children entered a trancelike state during these visitations, and only shared the messages with the rest of the village when the apparitions were finished.

When word of the visitations started to spread, hundreds of thousands of pilgrims began trekking to Medjugorje in the hopes of seeing the mother of Jesus and witnessing for themselves the great miracles that were occurring there.

For my parents—both devout Catholics who prayed regularly to the Virgin Mary—the apparitions seemed to be an answer to their prayers. People at church told them that several miracles had been seen in Medjugorje, such as the sun spinning in the sky above the tiny village. But there had also been reports that many pilgrims there had been cured of grave illnesses, ailments, and all manner of diseases and injuries.

Mom and Dad believed with all their hearts that if there was any chance, even the very remotest possibility, that making a pilgrimage to Medjugorje would miraculously heal me and make me whole again, then they had to act upon it at once. They decided that no matter what it took, they were going to get me to Yugoslavia.

My father is a loyal and caring family man who always worked to be the best possible provider he could be and ensure that his loved ones never wanted for anything. He really wanted to make the pilgrimage to Medjugorje, but he was busy with his insurance company.

Therefore, my parents agreed that Dad would stay home with my brothers and hold down the fort, and Mom would take me to Yugoslavia. Before long, we were off, traveling with a group of other Catholics who were on the same pilgrimage.

I was only seven years old, and I found my first trip out of the country to be both fascinating and frightening. Just traveling with my mother was a memorable experience in itself because we'd never really gone anywhere alone together, unless it was to a hospital for yet another surgery. But now we were making our way to an exotic country I'd never even heard of, and a place where the mother of Jesus was supposed to be visiting to boot! What an adventure, like setting off on a journey to a magical place from a storybook!

The reality was quite a bit different.

THE YUGOSLAVIAN COUNTRYSIDE was like an alien landscape to me, and just about as far away from our suburban American lifestyle as I could possibly imagine. To say that I was shocked as we arrived in the village would be an understatement. I was hungry when we got to Medjugorje; since I'd never been out of the country, I imagined that we'd find a McDonald's drive-through somewhere. Instead, we found cows and goats wandering through the middle of the street, along with chickens and roosters living in people's homes.

Mom and I stayed with a wonderfully warm and friendly family for our ten-day visit. However, they spoke very little English and were so poor that they didn't have electricity. It was winter by then, and my mother and I had to sleep fully clothed so we wouldn't freeze. In the evening, she and I sat around the family's fire to keep warm, and we all figured out a sort of sign language so we could communicate with each other. The family was very kind—and even if I wasn't accustomed to the living conditions or the local cuisine of lamb and peppers and salty cheeses, we had some laughs and shared some bonding meals together.

Every morning, Mom and I would hike up the mountain to the area where the young visionaries received their apparitions of Mary. Along the way, we'd see hundreds of people camping in tents outside in the freezing cold and whipping wind. When the afternoon arrived, the visionaries gathered in a little room at the home of a local priest and received their "visit." Each day, a different handful of people was invited into the special chamber to observe, and pray with, the visionaries while everyone else stood outside. My mother and I were among those invited on two separate occasions, and we watched the children with their upturned faces and shining eyes pray and talk to the Holy Mother. While neither Mom nor I saw or heard Mary or witnessed any of the so-called miracles—healing or otherwise—being there was still a very spiritual and profound experience.

When my mom and I returned to Louisiana, my body was exactly as it had been when we left. I hadn't undergone a miraculous healing or been supernaturally cured, but my parents were still certain that a change might come. So within the year, I was again on a jet flying over the Atlantic on my second visit to Medjugorje.

This time I traveled with my father, who was convinced that the second visit would be the charm. Dad and I prayed every day, but again, we didn't experience any miracles. We even went to a health spa in another remote Yugoslav village, where my father had been told that a wonder cream was being produced that doctors and hospitals throughout the region applied on burn victims with miraculous results. Allegedly, the cream had powerful curative properties when used regularly—the scars of even the most severely burned were said to magically disappear, leaving the victim's skin healthy, smooth, and whole.

My dad and I returned to the U.S. with six or seven big jars of the gooey ointment, which my parents faithfully applied to my body each day . . . that is, until my skin broke out in a rash and developed an infection. The "wonder" cream quickly ended up in the garbage.

Once again, a family member and I had come back from our Yugoslavian pilgrimage with no visible sign of a miracle. Yet although my skin was still scarred, my face was a mess, and my fingers hadn't grown back, that didn't mean my family hadn't been blessed. How could these trips *not* have been a blessing? After all, we allowed ourselves to be motivated by faith, love, and hope.

I also believe that traveling to Medjugorje had done two very important things: it strengthened the bond between my parents and myself, and it made me think long and hard about what it really meant to experience a miracle.

What I concluded (and again, much of my reasoning was on a subconscious level) was that if a miracle was going to happen to me, *I* was the one who was going to make it happen. It would still require a great act of faith, but the faith I'd need to have would be in myself—that is, in my own abilities to succeed in whatever I attempted, despite the physical obstacles I faced.

IN THE MONTHS FOLLOWING MY RETURN from Medjugorje, I doubled my efforts in all aspects of my life. I tried harder at school, I tried harder at sports, and I tried harder to master the biggest challenge of my young life—tying my shoelaces. Sure enough, I discovered something about myself that I still rely on to this day: by trying harder, putting in an extra effort, practicing, and giving my all to something, I make my own miracles happen. And as strange as it might sound, one of the first places I noticed my ability to make miracles happen was on the basketball court.

My parents encouraged me to play sports—with the exception of football. That's because my bones remained so brittle after the fire that one solid hit from an average-size linebacker more than likely would have shattered my arms, legs, and back. Fortunately, the parks and community centers in our area had all sorts of organized sports, and I became pretty skilled at many of them through the years. I was good at soccer and accomplished at baseball, but I excelled at basketball.

Dribbling or passing a basketball wasn't easy without hands, but I did pretty well by developing my own technique. More than anything, the key to playing well was practicing, and pushing myself to become as good as my body would allow. I competed with myself, and eventually that led me to become a very competitive child in everything from sports to academics. And of all the things I loved competing in, basketball was number one. Baseball was a close second, but B-ball was my passion—

I lived for the game, and I got better and better as the years went by.

When I first started in organized sports, the kids chosen to be team captains would pick me last to be on their team. It hurt my feelings, but I got used to it. If I put myself in their shoes, I guess I could understand their reasoning—who wanted someone with no hands at the plate when the bases were loaded? But when it came to basketball, I joined community leagues where the captains and coaches had to play every kid who tried out for the team.

When I'd get on the court and start to compete, it never failed to delight me when I saw the shocked looks on everyone's faces. Suddenly, they were all watching the kid with no fingers dribbling down the court with amazing speed, weaving through the defense, making incredible passes, or leaping and twisting through the air to make a basket on his own. Ha!

Smashing other people's preconceptions and prejudices was half the fun of playing. I mean, I'd been dealing with that kind of limited thinking my entire childhood. I loved proving to people that just because someone looked different, it didn't mean that he or she wasn't every bit as good a person, a student, or an athlete. I'd already made that "miracle" breakthrough in my mind and stopped seeing myself as limited, and now I started taking every opportunity to expand the narrow thinking of others. Back then the basketball court was not only a perfect place for me to prove myself, it was also a heck of a lot of fun.

By the time I was ten years old, I was playing point guard on our team in the local league. (Point guard, if you don't know, is a very important position—think Steve Nash or Magic Johnson.) I was very fast and had become pretty darn good on defense. It seemed that I could always find the open guy on the floor and get the ball to him with no problem.

We played a regional tournament game in which we were up against the best team in the league. Because I was point guard, I felt a tremendous sense of pride that I was leading my team in that particular match. But the point guard on the other team was a star player, one of the very best in his age group in southeastern Louisiana. I think because he saw that I had no hands, he felt like he could just dance around me, which he did for a while. By the end of the first quarter, the score was very one-sided—my team and I were being whooped badly, trailing by almost 20 points.

Our coach was trying to get us pumped up by telling us a motivational story about his team coming from behind to snatch victory from the jaws of defeat during his own days of playing basketball. He revved us all up and got us very excited; when we hit the court for the second quarter, I was determined to be part of the big comeback for our team. As soon as the quarter started, the opposition began pushing us hard. I was face-to-face with the point guard from the other team and stuck to him like glue. This time he didn't have a chance to show off his quickness and fancy ballhandling as he had in the first quarter. All he could do was dump the ball, which is exactly what we wanted him to do.

I played with an intensity I hadn't experienced since tackling my friend Kieran in kindergarten, and by half-time our teams were tied on the scoreboard. Later, during a pivotal moment in the game, the opposing team's point guard and I got into a bit of a scuffle. As we scrambled on the floor, we both went tumbling down in front of the crowd. We were taken out of the game to cool down, but now that the other point guard was off the floor, my team surged ahead! By the fourth quarter, we'd closed the gap, and the game could have gone either way.

We ended up losing by only two points, but I'd earned the respect of my fellow players. I'd showed my mettle in front of the crowd, and I'd also shown my teammates that I was indeed a valuable player. I'd stood my ground and hustled as best I could—even if it did get me tossed from the game! It was one of those moments I'll always look back upon with a certain level of pride, because I truly realized that no matter how I looked, I was going the distance.

A FEW DAYS AFTER THAT TOURNAMENT GAME, I got a phone call from *The Times-Picayune* newspaper, asking if they could do a feature on me. They'd heard about my efforts and decided that my story would make a good article.

A day or two later, a reporter interviewed me and my family at home and also went on to talk to my teachers and coaches. It was an amazing thing for a child who'd only recently stopped thinking that he was forever going to be mocked or shunned. I felt excited about the opportunity to tell my story and to talk about my family and my love for basketball.

After it appeared, the article opened up even more opportunities. Before long, I was asked to be the "King" of the children's Easter parade. As I sat on the throne they'd built atop the lead float, wearing a white tuxedo and crown, I waved at the throng of people who were crowding the sidewalks and waving back. I remember thinking that just a few years before I'd felt so lost, so alone, and so ignored. But now I could hear the cheers from the crowd all around me, the positive affirmations being given to me by complete strangers.

Naturally, my family was standing along the route as well, and I felt so much pride at having them there, knowing they'd been a driving force in my life. I was now where I was because my mother and father had stuck by me through thick and thin. They'd taught me to never give up, and it's a lesson I'd learned well.

On that day as I led the parade, I didn't feel the strange "surge" that I'd felt earlier in my life, but I did feel something close to it—and that was a sense of accomplishment and acceptance. I was no longer a target of discrimination; I was being embraced and accepted for who I was and celebrated for my achievements. Sitting on top of that float, I felt like the king of the world for a day—and that was truly incredible.

Soon after, I was made an honorary major in the Jefferson Parish Sheriff's Office. How life turns out! Harry Lee, the sheriff at the time, became a friend and went on to ask me to be in several Mardi Gras parades as his sidekick. There I was, dressed in a miniature police outfit and sitting beside Jefferson Parish's top cop! Sheriff Lee was also a local celebrity, which made the entire experience even more meaningful to me.

But while recognition and public acclaim can be remarkable, many miracles are small and happen at moments we never suspect. The greatest wonder of my childhood, for instance, came out of the blue after years of frustration and constant persistence.

Sitting on a bench after one particular gym class, I found myself staring down at my unlaced sneakers. As you already know, at the age of five I'd made it my life's mission to tie my own shoelaces. Now here I was years later, on the cusp of adolescence, and I had yet to master that simple act.

That day, alone on the bench, my most profound personal miracle occurred. I bent down and tied the pair of laces on my left shoe together into a bow. It certainly wasn't perfect, but it was there, and there was no denying it. Then I repeated the act on the right shoe. I didn't think or try—I just did it.

There was no fanfare or applause; what went through me at that moment was even bigger. Those few seconds of simple shoelace tying were the culmination, the embodiment, of every obstruction that I'd encountered up to that point in my life. So many years of struggle stopped cold as I looked down at my feet. Two tied shoes were staring up at me from the floor, and I'd tied them myself—a miracle of my own making.

♦ ♦ ♦

Chapter Five

The Gift of Music

Not long after I finally mastered tying my own shoe-laces, I was ready for an even greater challenge. I was almost 13 years old when I asked my father if he'd help me find a musical instrument I could learn to play.

Dad looked at me and smiled, as though he'd been waiting my whole life for me to ask that very question.

As I've mentioned, I come from a very musical background. Dad had been a professional trumpet player before he got married, his parents had both been musicians, and my older brothers each played an instrument—Johnny played trumpet like our dad, while Scott had taken up the trombone. And not only was it in my blood, it was in the air around me. Since I'd grown up in New Orleans, I'd been surrounded by music from the time I drew my very first breath. The city has spawned some of the greatest American musicians of all time, and the rhythms of Mardi Gras—the concerts, parades, and jazz festivals—were part of my very being.

When I was a kid, Dad always had an album spinning on the record player at home, usually a big band or a group with a huge horn section. I was weaned on Tower of Power and Blood, Sweat & Tears; and I knew who the members of the band Chicago were before I could even locate the Windy City on a map.

In addition, I can remember being very little and sitting on my father's knee as we watched TV in the living room. Whenever a show came on with a musical intro, such as *Bonanza,* Dad would use his fingertips to tap out the rhythm of the show's theme on my back or arm. Because he was a musician, the tapping he did was fairly intricate.

I'd always ask, "What are you doing on my back, Dad? What's that called?" He'd answer, "Oh, those are sixteenth notes, Danny," or "Those are what you call triplets." It didn't really matter *what* it was, though—I was fascinated by it. I'd make him explain how he did what he was doing, and then teach me how to do it myself.

Obviously, I'd been learning to play music from a very early age. Yet the thought of actually mastering an instrument with my burned-up hands had always been too intimidating for me to entertain—that is, until I tied my own shoes. Once I'd accomplished that, I felt I could do anything. If becoming a musician was what I was destined to do, as I believed it was, then looking down at my neatly tied laces told me I was now ready to fulfill that destiny.

So when I asked my father if he could help me find an instrument, we began the search immediately. The first thing we tried was the trumpet, as it had become a bit of a family tradition. However, like all other brass instruments, it came with a mouthpiece that required the player to shape his or her lips in a specific way to blow a steady stream of air into the horn. *My* lips had mostly burned away, and what was left or had been reconstructed simply wasn't up to the task. The same held true with forming a proper seal around the delicate reeds of woodwind instruments like the saxophone and clarinet, two instruments I loved listening to and desperately wished I could play.

Then our attention turned to the piano. My family had always had a beautiful, ornately carved piano in the house with gorgeous ivory keys that I'd fooled around with a million times. But when it came to sitting down and actually playing music, I was hopeless. Without fingers, I couldn't manipulate the keys in a way to make anything other than noise. There was the possibility of the guitar, but again, how would I form a decent-sounding chord without fingers? It quickly became obvious that any stringed instrument from the cello to the electric bass was, quite literally, beyond my grasp.

Dad and I spent hours trying to figure out how I could make music in a way that didn't require fingers or strong lips. Then he remembered how I used to ask him about the rhythms he'd tap out when we watched television. His eyes kind of lit up as he reminded me of this: "Danny, not only did you always want to know how I made different kinds of rhythms, but you used to bang on the pots and pans whenever you helped unload the dishwasher. Maybe we should get you a snare drum!"

And that was it.

THE NEXT SATURDAY MORNING, my father and I climbed into the car for what turned out to be one of the most significant days of my life. It was a beautiful fall morning as we pulled out of the driveway and headed downtown.

Dad pulled up in front of the same pawnshop we'd visited a week or two before when we'd gone shopping for a used trombone for my brother Scott. The store owner recognized us right away and ushered us in, pointing out a few different drum kits after Dad told him why we'd come back. While my father was highly enthusiastic about my taking up an instrument, he was cautious and frugal, too. He wasn't about to splurge on an entire drum kit, secondhand or not, until he knew if the drums would be a good fit for me and I'd take playing an instrument seriously. That day, he bought me a single snare drum and two drumsticks.

Dad didn't have to wait long to discover just how serious I was, though. From the minute he carried the snare to our den and set it up, I spent every spare minute I had banging away on it. I wouldn't call what I was doing at first making music, but I *was* making a connection with an instrument that would become part of my soul and express my thoughts and feelings as well as, or better than, words ever could.

But the very first time I whacked a drumstick across the taut skin of that just-purchased snare drum, I'm sure I looked more like a lumberjack hacking into a giant redwood than a fledgling drummer trying his best to emulate a percussion giant like Buddy Rich, or one of my other musical heroes. The trouble, as you might imagine, was this: I had no fingers or thumb to speak of on my right hand, and the thumb the doctors in Boston had constructed on my left hand had very little strength, certainly not enough to hold on to a drumstick with the necessary grip. Not all drum playing is beat and rhythm; it's also the technique with which you hold the sticks. I was swinging with all my might, but it didn't matter.

Pretty soon I gave up on the idea that I was going to play like a "normal" two-handed drummer—obviously I wasn't normal. As I'd done when I was learning to button my shirts, use utensils at the dinner table, or shoot hoops on the basketball court, I tossed out the regular playbook everyone else used to get through life and made up my own rules. I vowed that I would master the drums, just as I had mastered tying my shoes. It took me more than seven years before I tied my laces; thankfully, it took me less than seven weeks to figure out a way to play the drums without hands!

I began with my left hand, which had the reconstructed thumb. Actually, I had no problem gripping a drumstick between my engineered thumb and the remnants of my left hand. But as soon as I hit the drum itself, the stick would tumble out of my hand and go spinning to the ground. At first that was it—one hit, or two at the very most, and the stick was bouncing off the tiled floor.

Okay, that's not a problem, I thought. *If I can just hold on to the stick and make at least one complete swing, then all I have to do is practice. Sooner or later, I'll build up enough strength in my thumb to complete two full swings. And if I can do two swings, it's just a matter of time before I'll be slamming that stick against the drumhead 2,000 times in a row!*

The big issue for me was what to do with my right hand. No matter how many hours of physiotherapy I put in or how much I exercised it, there was basically no muscle on that hand for me to develop. There was no way I'd ever be able to use that nonhand and nonthumb to wield a drumstick. But somehow I had to make it work for me. If I was going to play professionally, I needed to use two drumsticks . . . so I had to get creative.

I put down the sticks and dedicated many long hours of thought to solving the problem. The most obvious solution was to somehow fasten the drumstick to my right wrist. The first thing I tried was a leather bowling glove. The glove fit over my wrist snugly, and the leather was rigid enough to keep the stick pressed against my lower arm when I hit the drum. I used the glove for about four or five days before I ripped it off in frustration.

It turns out that most of the stick would get buried in the glove, and the part that was exposed was too rigid to be of any good—the stick didn't move at all when I brought it down to the drumhead, and was about as flexible as a steel pipe. I'd quickly learned that to make a decent sound on the drums, the stick had to move freely in the drummer's hand. So, back to the drawing board I went.

The origin of the next idea I came up with stemmed from a childhood image of my mother standing in our kitchen attempting to repair a broken vase using Super Glue. Mom had accidentally spilled some of the adhesive on the inside of her arm and then somehow managed to get a large wooden stirring spoon stuck to her wrist. I remember watching her swing her arm around in the air to try to shake the spoon loose, but no matter how hard she tried to get rid of it, that spoon stuck to her like it was an extension of her arm. Eureka!

I headed off to the supermarket to buy myself a tube of Super Glue. Big mistake. While I did manage to adhere the drumstick to my wrist, a huge chunk of scar tissue and skin was ripped from my forearm the first time I hit the drum. My next idea, using heavy-duty duct tape, was as big a failure as the glue idea and just as painful. I also tried string, rope, and electrical cord.

After three weeks of trial and error, I was sitting in front of the snare drum when my dad noticed an old tennis wristband lying on the floor. He suggested I give it a try, which I did immediately. I found that the stretchy cotton was too flimsy to keep the drumstick in place—but it felt good on my arm, and that gave me the idea that would change my entire musical future.

I leapt up from my chair and ran to a drawer where we kept a bunch of rubber bands. I then hurried back to the snare, winding a couple of the rubber bands over the top of the tennis wristband as I went. When I sat back down in front of the drum, I slipped the drumstick under the wristband and swung my right arm up just past my ear, and then I brought my arm down to the drumhead with all my might. The drumstick hit the skin and made a sound, a beautiful musical note, which I'll never forget.

I hit it again and again and again: *Thwack! Thwack! Thwack!* My father let out a loud cheer, and so did I. We'd just found the method that would allow me to make music and eventually become a professional drummer.

The rubber-band-and-tennis-wristband technique worked so perfectly from the very start that I haven't modified it at all since the day I discovered it. I've had some of the top orthopedic and plastic surgeons in the country suggest other methods, and even had several occupational therapists design prosthetic devices to try to improve my drumming technique, but nothing has ever worked better than a cheap cotton wristband and rubber bands from the kitchen drawer.

Once I had my right-handed problem solved, I launched into playing with both hands every single day. I practiced hour after hour, until my shoulders ached and my arms felt as though they'd fall off. Each morning I could tell that the thumb the doctors had built for me on my left hand was just a little bit stronger than it had been the day before. And sure enough, when I started playing that day, I'd be able to hit the skin of the snare drum another five or six more times than I had the day before. I was on my way!

My mother was happy that I'd found something I loved doing so much, but I know that she would have preferred I'd found a less noisy hobby . . . perhaps stamp collecting, or maybe mime! But my father, a dyed-in-the-wool musician, couldn't have been more pleased by the way I threw myself into making music.

Dad didn't hear a racket when I practiced; he heard my passion . . . and he heard improvement. When it became obvious to him that I wasn't going to give up on the drums, he invited an old buddy of his to drop by the house and listen to me play. His name was Glenn

Diecedue, and he became both a good friend and my first drum teacher.

GLENN HAD BEEN A PROFESSIONAL DRUMMER for years and had gigged with everyone in New Orleans. He'd performed at all the big jazz clubs in the French Quarter, toured with different groups, sat in on recording sessions, and even played on riverboats up and down the Mississippi. Although he originally came over to the house to help me out as a favor to my dad, I couldn't have asked for a better first teacher.

Glenn knew how serious I was about drumming and that I dreamed of being a professional. He was straight with me right from the start. "Listen to me, Danny," he said during our first lesson, before I'd even picked up my drumsticks. "Being a drummer is tough. There are a million guys trying to do the same thing as you, and they've got their hands. For someone like you, it's going to be unbelievably hard.

"I'm telling you right now, don't worry about what other people say. If you're going to be a drummer, you have to focus on the music, and you have to play for yourself. You're never going to be like any other drummer, so don't try to copy anyone else . . . if you're going to succeed, you're going to have to find your own technique, invent your own style. That's what I'll try to help you do."

That was some of the best musical advice I ever received, and I took it to heart.

Glenn was hugely encouraging. He often told me that I had genuine talent and urged me to practice as much as possible. He came by the house once a week and showed me all the basics, such as stick control and how to read music. He also set up a regimented practice routine that not only tripled the pace at which I was learning, but built up the strength in my arms and thumb as well, which allowed me to work twice as hard.

Just three months into my lessons with Glenn, I was holding the stick in my left hand for minutes at a time, rather than seconds. And the wristband that had at first seemed a bit awkward as it pressed the stick against my right arm soon felt like it was a part of my body. I was improving so rapidly that I was growing frustrated at only being able to practice on the single snare drum my father had bought me at the pawnshop.

Sensing my impatience, Glenn had a little chat with my dad. Not long afterward, my teacher showed up at our house with one of his old drum kits for me to use. "They're yours, kid," he said with a smile.

My creative world, which had been limited to the rhythms I could tap out on a solitary drumhead, had just exploded into a universe of possibilities. Instead of focusing all my energy on one lonely snare drum, I now had a bass drum, a floor tom, an extra snare, and tom-toms to whale on; not to mention the shiny brass crash, hi-hat, and ride cymbals that were suddenly at my command. I was euphoric that day . . . but my poor mother! The noise that began echoing through our house that day didn't stop until I moved out years later to go to college.

Glenn also helped me set up a stereo system, which allowed me to practice along with the recordings of some of my favorite songs and musicians. Soon my father and older brothers were coming by for impromptu jam sessions—Dad would play trumpet or harmonica, Johnny would play second trumpet, and Scott rocked on with his trombone. My baby brother, Paul, who was just four or five years old at the time, would sit on the floor clapping his hands and humming as we jammed.

After several months of drum lessons and hundreds of hours of practice, I felt that I had a fairly solid understanding of the fundamentals of drumming. The following year, my family moved to another town where I'd begin high school. My drumming skills were so developed by then that in my freshman year, the band director gave me sheet music that only the most advanced seniors were using. Because I started my new school in September, I'd missed the summer band program. Consequently, I wasn't allowed to be in the varsity marching band, and could only play in the school's beginner band. But by the next year, I'd auditioned for the varsity band and was made both first chair and section leader of the band, a position I'd keep all the way through my high-school years.

I kept on practicing, both at home and at school. When I was in the concert band, I'd often play the enormous kettledrums (or timpani), which make such a deep and sonorous sound that I felt as tall and powerful as an oak tree when I struck them. And during football games, I'd parade along with the marching band under the bright floodlights illuminating the fall sky, playing four-piece quad drums (or tenor drums, as they're sometimes called) in front of hundreds of cheering parents and students. Not bad for a kid who at the beginning of his academic career had been heckled by his kindergarten classmates and called a monster.

Meanwhile, Glenn and I continued our weekly sessions, and I kept improving. He even invited me to sit in and play with a real jazz band he belonged to during a local music festival. When he first asked, I was dubious; as the date approached, I became so nervous that I thought I'd forgotten how to breathe. So I just applied a lesson I'd already learned in the past—practice, practice, practice. Long before I took to the stage, I got ahold of the music we were to play and practiced it every morning and night until I was practically playing it in my sleep.

When the time came for the outdoor festival, I took my place on the raised platform with Glenn and the other musicians and took a deep breath. I knew I was prepared, and that made me feel confident I'd hold my own—which I did, and then some. During that short but successful public debut, I felt something like the energy that had gone through me that day in kindergarten when I felt myself open up to the universe in the school yard . . . and it made me hungry for more.

I'd thrown myself into my music—practiced and prepared—with the passion of a man certain that this was his destiny. The applause that washed over me when I left the stage that day is still part of who I am. From that moment forward, I knew with certainty that whatever I did in the future, my success would be determined by how seriously I approached the work.

I'D BEEN PLAYING THE DRUMS for a little over a year when I received a call from a segment producer on *The Montel Williams Show* in New York City. It seems that Montel was doing a program about young people who had been burned or disfigured but had come to terms with their injuries and had gone on to lead normal, productive lives.

The producer asked if I was interested in appearing on the show with other young "survivors"; if so, Montel would fly me and one of my parents to the Big Apple, put us up in a fancy hotel in Times Square, and arrange for a limo to take us to and from the studio. The show would be taped the next afternoon, which happened to be my 14th birthday.

I talked it over with my parents, and we agreed that if sharing my story on national television might help other kids struggling with the kind of difficulties I'd experienced, then I should definitely do it. So the next morning, Mom and I were in a Boeing 747 circling the Manhattan skyline as the pilot waited for the go-ahead to land at JFK International Airport. It was a bizarre and exciting journey, and our first big mother-son trip since returning from Yugoslavia seven years earlier.

That afternoon I was on the set of *Montel* sharing my story, doing my best to encourage others who were burned not to be discouraged or allow their injuries to get in the way of their dreams. To bring home the point I was trying to make, the producers rolled some home video that my mom had brought from Louisiana, which showed me playing the drums. After we finished taping, I received a nice surprise when Montel and the producers presented me with a birthday cake.

But my biggest surprise came later, when I saw how my story acted as a powerful tool in the lives of others. Since that show aired in 1993, dozens of complete strangers have stopped me on the street in cities all over the country to thank me for going on *Montel*. They've told

me that seeing me play the drums without hands motivated them to follow their own dreams, despite whatever
obstacles life had put in their way. After I'd heard a few
stories like that, I realized that the *real* gift of music was
its ability to inspire others.

◆ ◆ ◆

Chapter Six

Navigating the
High-School Waters

As much as I was inspired by being on *Montel* and had enjoyed my 15 minutes of fame in the national spotlight, I was also entering a phase of my life where I often wished that I could crawl under a rock and hide from the world. That phase was called *high school*.

By the time I hit adolescence, I was painfully aware that I'd never be part of a popular clique. I certainly wasn't going to be a jock—even though I could play many sports well—and I wasn't going to be a preppy or part of the cool crowd. No, I was going to be what I'd been for most of my life: "different looking." That knowledge didn't do me a lot of good, though; it definitely didn't give me any insight into how to live a normal life, deal with girls, or ignore the gawkers and morons who laughed at me when I was out in public.

Whatever hassles and heartaches I'd experienced in my young life were intensified during high school. Much later I'd come to recognize and appreciate the spiritual gifts I'd received as a result of being burned. But during the majority of my teenage years, it was very difficult for me to see beyond what I'd lost.

As I BEGAN MY FRESHMAN YEAR, at least I knew with certainty that the one thing I could do was play drums. I cultivated the ever-growing sensation inside of me that one day I could and would be a fine drummer—maybe even a *great* drummer! That knowledge is what I held on to whenever I faced new challenges—such as entering high school in a new town.

Just a few months prior, my parents had decided that it was time for the family to relocate. The neighborhood my brothers and I had grown up in was changing rapidly; we'd had a population explosion in the area that had brought in a lot of petty crime, quasi-gang activity, and drug dealing to what had once been a peaceful family suburb. When I was three or four years old, I remember listening to crickets as I fell asleep . . . seven or eight years later, the most frequent sounds coming through my bedroom window at night were gunshots and police sirens.

So we moved about 40 miles out of town (which I considered the sticks), where we could see giant pine trees swaying in the breeze and once again hear crickets in the evening air. The town was called Mandeville, a small commuter community on the north side of Lake Pontchartrain. New Orleans proper sits on the south side of the huge lake, which is the second largest saltwater lake in America after Utah's Great Salt Lake.

Although we weren't that far away from New Orleans, that big body of water did a good job of cutting us off from the people we'd grown up with. This meant that when my brothers and I arrived in our new hometown, we didn't know a single soul.

To make matters worse, I had to take the bus to get to school. From kindergarten until eighth grade, my mother had always driven me, so I never had to worry about sitting next to other kids on the bus. Now that had all changed. In many ways, I was facing the world on my own for the very first time.

Of course, it was high time for me to board a school bus just like every other kid did. By now, I was old enough and confident enough (or getting there, anyway) to handle whatever the other boys and girls might dish out. And handle it I did. A lot of times the seats around me on those first bus trips stayed vacant. But after a while—after I'd gotten to be friends with a few of the kids—those seats filled up.

I was also lucky that my big brother Scott was in his senior year when we arrived in Mandeville, and we'd often go to school together. (By this point, my eldest brother, Johnny, was off to college, so I didn't see him too much. I didn't see much of my little brother, Paul, either, because he was just starting elementary school.)

Once Scott and I clamored off the bus with all the other kids, however, we'd separate for the rest of the day. He'd go off to his classes, and I'd go off to mine and be on my own all day long.

IT MAY HAVE BEEN IN THE STICKS, but Mandeville High School was huge to me. I'd come from a private school where the student body consisted of 200 kids at the very most, and my new public school had more than 2,000! The size difference was so overwhelming for me that just being at that school was physically and emotionally exhausting. Often I'd find myself fighting upstream against a river of students flowing around me while I was heading in the opposite direction; pushing my way around or through groups of kids gathered into little hallway roadblocks, gabbing and gossiping between classes; or lugging 20 or 30 pounds of books across the enormous campus, which seemed larger than most small cities to me.

At least during my first day, which was dedicated to orientation, I was able to meet a few upperclassmen who'd been assigned to show me around and make me as comfortable in my new surroundings as they could. But then I was left to deal with the problems, perils, and emotional pitfalls of high-school life by myself—such as negotiating the cafeteria.

Lunch was held during two different periods, one for juniors and seniors, the other for the freshmen and sophomores. This meant I wouldn't get to eat with those nice upperclassmen or my brother Scott.

Those first few weeks enduring the noon-hour meal were pretty much hell, if you want to know the truth. I'd sit in the center of one of the long institutional dining tables, and no one would sit anywhere near me. It was as though the other students suspected that my scars were contagious, that somehow they'd get burned by sitting too close to me! Just like in kindergarten, I could almost feel their stares as they choked down their sandwiches. And just like in kindergarten, the kids grew bolder, and their snickers and nasty whispering became loud enough for me to hear.

For example, when there were no other open seats one day, a ninth-grade boy standing a few inches away from me loudly asked his friend: "You must be joking! Do I *have* to sit by him?" I focused my attention on the food tray in front of me and kept eating my meal. What else could I do? If you're swimming in a pool filled with hungry sharks, the last thing you want to do is let them know you're bleeding. Sure, these types of remarks hurt deeply, but I did my best to ignore them and protect myself by forming a sort of scar tissue over my heart, as I already had over most of my body.

Soon I developed a kind of inner radar that picked up on the people in a crowd most likely to attack or insult me. To this day I remain highly sensitive to the energy flow of others and get a sense of how they're going to react to me before they know what their reaction is going to be themselves—I call it "vibing" people. While I used to rely on this as a tool for protecting my own emotions, more and more I employ it to protect other individuals from embarrassing themselves.

These days I'm more sympathetic to strangers who react rudely when they first meet me. I understand they have issues and fears of their own that make them act out defensively. But back in high school, I wasn't nearly as sophisticated in my thinking. So when a fellow student lashed out at me with his or her tongue, it really stung.

Thank God I had my drum set. As soon as I returned home after school, I could retreat to the den, break out my sticks, and go crazy. For a long time I used the drums as a release for the hurt and frustration that was part of my daily life. Anger was such a part of my drumming style that I became a very aggressive player and often played like a real beast. In fact, one of my nicknames on the drums is "Danimal."

But I'm happy to say that I've left much of that way of playing in the past, where it belongs. I'm still a very aggressive drummer, but I never let anger fuel my performance anymore. I have far too much respect for the instrument and for the music to do that. Besides, I've learned that when you allow anger—which is an emotion based in ego—to dominate any aspect of your life, you're closing yourself off to love. And love is the most positive and creative artistic force in the universe. Again, these were all things I'd learn further down the road of life; during high school, I needed every outlet I could find to vent my anger and keep myself sane.

It was also helpful that Scott, who was a senior, had made friends fairly easily and introduced me to some of the boys he'd met. I also became acquainted with some older students on my own through gym class. You see, for the most part, my skin doesn't have pores. This means that I am extremely sensitive to the sun and have a difficult time regulating my core body heat. Since freshman and sophomore physical-education classes generally consisted of outdoor activities—in the bright Louisiana sun!—the teachers arranged for me to be a part of the junior gym classes, which tended to take place in the gym. There I met those few whom I came to consider my pals.

I found all of these older kids much easier to hang out with because they were more mature and didn't feel the need to prove themselves by putting people down. When

I listened to them talk, I felt less lonely and put upon by my own classmates.

Sometimes when Scott's buddies dropped by the house, I'd flip through the books they brought over. Some of them featured stories of people and history that stirred something within me, making me think about myself as being part of a larger world for the first time. And it was through books that I made one of my first good friends at Mandeville High.

Her name was Mrs. Plesch, and she was my English teacher that first year. After she'd read an essay I wrote about rock 'n' roll and society, we began to talk quite a bit. She spoke to me differently, prodding me to think about things such as music and life. She was open to new philosophies and fresh ways of thinking. Through our daily chats after class, I too began to form my own awareness as to what I wanted to become. Looking back now, I see that thanks to her, I had a social outlet—and that was one of the things that saved me from the depths of total social abandonment.

ALTHOUGH I'D MADE A FEW FRIENDS during those first few months of school, I had yet to make any who were more or less my same age.

Then one day that changed. It happened in the lunchroom, of course. A big burly kid walked right over to me, tossed his tray down on the table, and sat across from me. He looked at me for a moment with great intensity and started a conversation.

"What happened to you?" he asked.

"I was burned in a fire when I was young."

"How old were you?"

"I was two."

"Damn. That must suck. Did it hurt?"

"I don't really remember any pain," I said.

He kept asking questions relating to my accident, and then he introduced himself: "I'm Matt. What are you doing over here all alone?"

"My name is Dan. I don't really have any friends," I admitted. "I'm not sure that anyone likes me . . . except a few of the older kids and my English teacher."

"Well, you've got a friend now. What do you do?"

I didn't understand the question. "What do you mean, what do I do?"

"I mean, do you like to do stuff?" Matt asked. He kept jamming food into his mouth and chewing kind of loudly. I suspected that he might be a bit of a ball-breaker and was maybe trying to show me up in front of the other students, but he seemed genuinely nice. He was also kind of funny.

"I play drums."

Matt's gaze shot directly down to the ends of my arms—which didn't look like any he'd ever seen before, obviously, especially on a drummer. "Get the hell out of here!" he exclaimed after a few seconds. "How do you do that? I don't know anything about the drums, but I play a little guitar, and I have a hard enough time doing that with *all* my fingers! I can't imagine playing without hands. Come on, man, you're putting me on! How the hell can you manage to ever hold on to drumsticks without any hands?"

"I do okay," I said, smiling at his openness. "I use a wristband to attach one stick to my right hand, and I can hold the other stick with my thumb on my left hand."

I held it up, wiggling my surgeon-constructed digit for him.

He whistled softly and shook his head in amazement. "Man, oh man! That is so cool . . . are you any good?"

I always hated it when someone asked me that. How was I supposed to respond? I settled on: "I'm okay, I guess."

That was all it took for us to become friends—me responding to Matt with an honest answer, and him not being freaked out by the way I looked. We began hanging out together quite a lot, both at school and after. At first we mainly hung at my house, jamming on instruments with my brothers and generally having a good time while getting to know each other. Matt would bring his guitar, and I'd play along with him on the drums. They were good days for me, uplifting and eye-opening.

Matt also knew a lot of people. He had one of those open faces and easy, likable personalities that attracted friends; I really looked up to him. Through him I got to know several other great people, and my life began to open up socially. Sometimes I couldn't believe what had been inside of me, but untapped, for so long—the ability to have good friendships!

It felt incredible to finally have someone around me (who was not my family member) who acted and behaved in a "normal" way around me. Maybe I'd been on the defensive for so long because I'd grown used to feeling isolated, as if it was my normal way to feel. Now that I was venturing out into the world, meeting Matt's buddies and making new pals on my own, that sense of seclusion was peeling away. I was extremely thankful to Matt, and attentive to the gift of friendship in my life. Matt Rycyk was (and still is) a solid guy, and an outstanding friend.

I did have to overcome a familiar hurdle not too long after we met, though. Matt took me over to his house, and his mother greeted me with a comforting hug. We then wandered into the next room, where his father sat reading the newspaper. I guess he was fairly engrossed in the paper because when he glanced up to acknowledge my introduction, the first thing out of his mouth was, "Nice mask." It wasn't a joke. He just hadn't been thinking . . . or perhaps he really did think I was wearing a mask. I honestly don't know.

Matt's mom almost died of embarrassment. As for me, I couldn't believe what I'd heard. I tried to chuckle a bit, not knowing what to do or say. My friend just sort of stood there, dumbfounded as well. Finally, after a couple of minutes of this awkward situation, Mrs. Rycyk explained to her husband, "Dear, he's not wearing a mask. This is Dan. He was burned in a fire when he was a little boy."

Mr. Rycyk, I knew, must have been in a personal hell when he realized what had just transpired. He was clearly upset by what had come out of his mouth and dropped his paper to take a second look at me. Then he got up and left the room without saying another word. I guess that's all he could do to try to save "face" after he'd inadvertently insulted mine. Mrs. Rycyk followed her husband out of the room, tossing a little glance of apology in my direction.

Matt and I, more or less, allowed the moment to move over us like an out-of-place rain cloud on an otherwise bright day. As I recall, he kind of rolled his eyes as if to

Celebrating my
second birthday
in our backyard,
November 16, 1981.

Playing around as a toddler.

At age two, dressed as a cowboy.

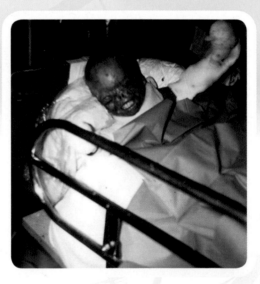

At the Shriners Hospital for Children in Boston shortly after the accident, June 1982.

Playing outside
Shriners Hospital.

With my mom
and constant
companion,
Marilyn.

Out whale watching while on a day pass from Shriners Hospital
for Children in Boston.

Celebrating my fifth birthday at Shriners Hospital, a few days after one of my surgeries.

Enjoying Christmas with my two older brothers, Johnny (on my shoulder) and Scott, 1983.

With my good pals Pluto and Dumbo, 1985.

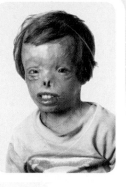

An early passport photo.

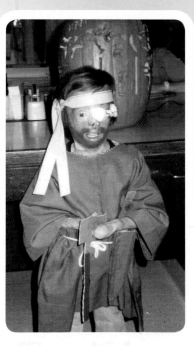

Dressing up as Rambo for
Halloween, 1985.

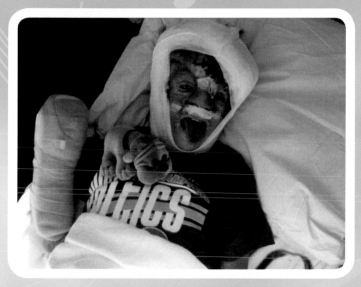

After yet another of my countless reconstructive surgeries at Shriners Hospital, 1986.

On a road trip with my big brothers, Johnny (left) and Scott.

In the classroom at age ten. Although I'd mastered the art of writing without fingers, it would take another two years before I could tie my own shoelaces. *(Photo by Susan Poag, © 2009 The Times-Picayune Publishing Co., all rights reserved. Used with permission of <u>The Times-Picayune</u>.)*

The "big game"! Squaring off against an opponent on the basketball court. *(Photo by Susan Poag, © 2009 The Times-Picayune Publishing Co., all rights reserved. Used with permission of <u>The Times-Picayune</u>.)*

Easter 1990, when I was crowned King of the Parade.

With Jefferson Parish Sheriff Harry Lee.

My official school picture, age 12.

At my eighth-grade graduation from Terrytown Academy, 1993.

With other guests of *The Montel Williams Show*, 1993.

Acting crazy and goofing around at home in 1994.

Celebrating my 15th birthday with my younger
brother, Paul.

My 1997
high-school
graduation
photo.

Playing at the world famous Tipitina's in New Orleans with the
band Dimorphodon.

Playing at the French Quarter Festival in New Orleans with the band Michael Ray & the Cosmic Krewe, 2003.

Speaking at the 2003 Shriners International convention in Minneapolis. My parents, John and Marilyn, are right behind me.

In front of my Brooklyn apartment with my dog, Dixie.

Playing at a local nursing home with my dad (on the trumpet) and some friends in 2007.

With my friend Wayne Dyer in Tampa, October 2008.

say, "Parents! What are you going to do?" And then we headed off in the direction of his room to check out his music collection.

♦ ♦ ♦

Chapter Seven

Finding My Own Way

School began to improve for me socially after the first semester. Students who'd heard me playing drums respected how serious I was about my music, and I made a few more good friends through the Mandeville High junior band. Music had a way of cutting through a lot of the social stigma that had always surrounded me. It wasn't long before my brother Scott and I formed a band called Rain Dogs with a few friends.

I was loving music more and more. I started listening to all kinds of bands and genres that, I'm embarrassed to say, I'd never really heard before. The Beatles, Pink Floyd, Led Zeppelin, and Jimi Hendrix are just some of the artists I "discovered" during this period; and their music had a profound effect on my psyche, as it did for the generations that came before me.

I started reading books about the hippie movement back in the '60s and found myself identifying with that whole culture of protests and questioning established values. My brother did, too, and often our views about music and society meshed perfectly.

What *wasn't* meshing perfectly for me anymore was the drudgery of school. Topics I used to find interesting—which was just about everything—now seemed stilted and boring, and my grades started slipping. I simply stopped caring about what "the establishment" was telling me I had to learn. I knew for sure that I wanted to steer my life toward music and was eager to learn everything about music history, music theory, and playing the drums. But as Frank Sinatra, the most celebrated crooner of my grandparents' generation, so famously sang, I wanted to do it my way.

I was becoming a bit of a rebel, which is often par for the adolescent course. My parents, however, weren't at all happy when it came to my declining grade point average and nonchalant attitude toward schoolwork. It wasn't unusual for me to be grounded for having blown off an essay or for getting into trouble in some other way at school. I was also not shy about blurting out my opinions on whatever social issue I'd convinced myself I suddenly knew more about than anyone else.

In my head, I was a "revolutionary." But really, I was just a normal teenager in a not-so-normal body, with some pretty atypical issues to deal with. I needed to flex my intellectual muscles, assert my independence, and test the waters of freethinking individuality. In my mind, that included toying with a little marijuana and booze, partly to make things interesting, and partly to deal with some emotional pain I still hadn't come to terms with.

I made darn sure that my parents didn't get wind of this particular side of my rebellion—they would have gone ballistic if they'd known—so I became sneaky and learned how to cover my tracks. I think I pulled it off, but then again, my mother and father are very smart people. What I do know for sure is that I was never dumb enough to let either one of them catch me red-handed with a joint! I was grounded plenty of times, but never for doing anything that would have broken my parents' hearts.

SCOTT AND I SPENT A LOT OF TIME playing with our band. We practiced at least twice a week, usually at one of our bandmate's homes—whoever could convince his parents to let us have loud jam sessions in their garage that week. When our parents were out of town, my brother and I would invite friends over and have late-night jams at our house. We actually got pretty good as a band and developed a small but faithful following in the area; we'd play at house parties, community centers, coffee shops, and the occasional benefit or battle of the bands.

I began to feel incredibly connected to the Rain Dogs and to the idea that I was really contributing something to the world. I was actually creating art, which reverberated within me as something truly important. This was an ability that was all my own and had absolutely nothing to do with the trauma I'd suffered as a child.

The art of the music was mine, and when I played in the band or even just hung out with the friends who came to our gigs or rehearsals, I felt alive in a way I never had before. It had to do with being part of something creative that was actually outside of my own body. My "sound" was part of my essence—it was truly in me as a striving artist—and floated up and out across the room in the form of a great beat, a rocking rhythm, and a fleeting piece of beautiful music. My art was making people happy.

While I may not have been thriving academically, I did begin to develop musically at Mandeville High. Not only was I playing drums with the junior band and constantly performing with the Rain Dogs, I also began seeking out and landing gigs with other bands when they needed a drummer to pinch-hit.

After I sat in on a gig with my drumming teacher, Glenn, everything started to mushroom—I was getting calls to play for bands all around the area, with musicians who were 20 to 30 years older than I was. This was quite different from jamming with a bunch of teenage boys. I was playing with real, professional musicians and hitting my drums to some of the greatest jazz standards ever written!

It was heady stuff, and at first I was intimidated by the thought of playing with such high-caliber performers with so much experience and expertise. Some of these older men were apprehensive about me at first, too, because of my age and the fact that I was a handless drummer! But in the end, they just wanted to make sure I could play at their level—and after they saw how I handled myself in the throes of a hot jam session, they accepted me.

It was strange, but I fit in with these guys as though I'd been playing for decades, not just a few years. They'd call me out of the blue to sub for a drummer who couldn't make it that night, and I was there, drumsticks in hand (so to speak). As a developing musician, it was an enormously educational experience to play rock 'n' roll one night with a bunch of teenagers, and then jazz standards the next with a group of seasoned pros. I learned how to handle myself no matter who or what the crowd was, and that knowledge couldn't have come at a better time.

FOR SOME TIME, I'D HAD A GROWING FEELING that I needed something spiritual in my life, which my parents' religion could not fulfill. Along with questioning established authority, I couldn't help but question what the Catholic Church and my parents had taught me to believe. I came to a point where I'd had enough of my family's morning prayers and going to church. When it got right down to it, I no longer felt the least bit like a committed Catholic.

Catholicism had obviously been a huge part of my formative years, and it had long been the pillar of my parents' beliefs. We had prayed the rosary as a family every morning since I could remember, seldom missed Mass on Sunday, and had made two trips to an apparition site in Yugoslavia to pray for the Virgin Mary to miraculously make my ruined body whole. We were most definitely a Catholic family! Yet as I discovered other philosophies and expanded my intellectual and artistic sensibilities, I was forced to take a hard look at what being Catholic meant to me.

For a while, I was confused about my identity. On one level I was an up-and-coming "hippie" idealist/musician; on another, I was an anxious young man who couldn't even attract the attention of a girl. I was continually tormented when it came to the opposite sex and felt doomed to be alone and without love forever.

As I sank into darkness, I sought further refuge in substances. Alcohol and marijuana were my drugs of choice, and I became very reckless and self-destructive. This all coincided with my rebellion against Catholicism . . . and whenever someone starts to question his faith, it ultimately comes down to his perception of his personal self-worth.

I bemoaned my fate, wondering why God had chosen me to live a life of misery. It didn't make sense that I'd been so badly burned, and seemed incredibly unfair. I cursed God for causing me so many years of pain—for inflicting such suffering on me when I was a small, helpless, innocent child. The more I dwelled on how unjust God had been, the more time I spent drinking, getting high, and staying awake all night wrestling with questions that had no answers.

Finally, I listened to my gut and asserted my independence: I stopped going to Mass altogether, breaking free from the Catholic Church. At first the break left me even more alone and confused, and I tumbled down into the depths of my own sorrow.

I know now that all of my inner battles about whether God was to blame for what happened to me were not only silly, but they were a colossal waste of energy. The only thing my negative thinking accomplished was to drag me deeper into the quicksand of self-pity and despair. The more I fought against what had happened to me in the past, the more I sank.

The simple answer is that there is never a way to turn back the clock. There is only the constant beat of forward movement. After a few years, this is what I came to know and understand. The biggest lesson life would eventually teach me is that there really are no negatives—every experience is simply an opportunity, and what we do with it determines if it helps or hurts us.

If someone had told me in the midst of my adolescent struggles that I'd choose to be burned as a child in order to learn valuable lessons, I would have laughed in his face (or better yet, punched him in the nose). And yet today, I'm convinced that the life I have is the life I chose for myself. But we all have to travel our own winding paths to make such discoveries, and in high school, I was still finding my way.

While I may not have become known as a young radical or my school's resident philosopher, I did earn a reputation as a talented drummer and solid musician; and that reputation opened new doors for me socially, academically, and professionally.

DURING MY SOPHOMORE YEAR, hundreds of other students from Mandeville High and I had to move to another school with the very Louisianan name of Fontainebleau. It turns out that our old school was bursting at the seams with an overflow of students. Fontainebleau High School was a brand-new facility—and in many ways, it was a brand-new start for me.

Unlike my old high school, Fontainebleau offered a special program designed for gifted music students, and I was accepted into its very first class . . . of which I was the only boy. What's more, I was only the second drummer allowed into a specialized program in the entire school district. As ridiculous as it sounds, drummers had not been thought capable of comprehending the intense music-theory aspect of such a class. And when the administrators saw me, with my particular "restrictions," they wondered if I'd handle the compulsory class requirement of playing at least some basic piano chords. Clearly, I had no fingers, and that ruled out the piano. But my teacher, Mrs. Rebecca Gillan, fought hard to get me into that program, and she won.

So there I was, Danny Caro: a gifted young drummer with star potential; a newly minted doubting Catholic; and a teenage boy with surging hormones, the only boy in a prestigious music class full of pretty teenage girls.

Adding to my teenage angst was the fact that Fontainebleau High School was so new that it was still under construction. This meant that some of the classrooms, including our music room, hadn't been fully finished when the students arrived. So for the first year, the gifted music class was held in a small utility room essentially the size of a large walk-in closet. I spent every class snugly surrounded by five girls who were all exceedingly talented, nice, and (did I mention?) attractive!

For the most part, these girls didn't seem to mind that I looked different from any other boy they'd ever seen. I had only two-thirds of my hair, I didn't have hands, and my entire face was completely scarred. I'm guessing they must have assumed that the rest of my body had been burned just as horribly as the parts they could see (but as I've mentioned, I was wearing a soggy diaper when I was caught in the explosion, so I'm happy to report that some very important parts of me remain completely undamaged).

Even though my classmates didn't look like they wanted to flee in horror every time I entered that tiny classroom, as some people have when forced into close proximity with me, none of them seemed interested in taking things beyond friendship. And at first that was just fine. The class was so small, and we worked so intimately together as a group, that a student romance could have ruined the class dynamic. On top of that, ever since an incident with a girl named Mandy in the fourth grade, I'd been hesitant to approach a member of the opposite sex for fear they'd reject or laugh at me—or do both.

MANDY WAS THE VERY FIRST GIRL I ever had a crush on, and to my young eyes, she was the most beautiful creature ever to have drawn breath. She sat directly across from me and had silky-smooth, shiny brown hair that cascaded across her shoulders and flowed halfway down her back. Her eyes were the deep, rich brown of darkened chestnuts; and I felt my stomach do little flips when she looked in my direction. For much of that year, I could only think and talk about Mandy.

By that time I had made friends with many of the kids at Terrytown Academy, was doing well academically, and held my own in any impromptu playground games of basketball or tag. I was a popular student, much more so than Mandy. Because she was also kind of shy, I guess I figured that would make me a shoo-in for her affection. I was sure I had a good shot at becoming her boyfriend, but I wanted to play my cards just right. So I kept my crush a secret until the perfect moment presented itself for me to reveal to her what was in my heart.

After Christmas, I was flipping through the family calendar on the kitchen wall when it hit me. The perfect moment for me to profess my love had already been determined: February 14.

With some friends' encouragement, I designed a personal Valentine's Day card for Mandy. As carefully as I could without hands, I drew pictures of flowers all over the yellow cardboard paper I'd selected for the special occasion. Then I wrote a little poem to go along with the drawing: *Roses are red / Violets are blue / But none of these pretty flowers are as beautiful as you!*

On the morning of the special day, I made sure to be in class before anyone else so that I could slip the card discreetly to Mandy as soon as she sat down at her desk. I was so nervous and excited that I couldn't look at her all morning. I figured she'd come up to me at recess to thank me for my gift, but when the bell rang, the object of my affection was up from her seat and out the classroom door without so much as a glance in my direction.

When I went outside, I spotted Mandy by the swing set she liked to hang out at with her friends. I saw that she was with a group of five or so girls, who were standing in a circle and passing my card around. Each time someone saw the card, a fresh peal of laughter would rise up above the playground.

I hung back out of sight until the bell rang and the girls went back to class. Once they were gone, I went over to the swings and found what was left of my Valentine's Day offering lying in a hundred pieces in the mud. After her friends had taken turns laughing at it, Mandy had shredded my gift and stomped it into the ground.

Heartbroken, I went back to class and took my seat across from Mandy. I looked to her for some kind of explanation, but none ever came. That girl never so much as looked at me again, even though we sat near each other. Fortunately, she moved away the following year, but she left an indelible mark on my heart.

So by the time I reached high school, I was understandably uncomfortable around girls my own age and fearful of showing my feelings. Yet the young women in the gifted music class were so nice to me that I began to feel more at ease in their presence and ended up becoming friends with all of them. We studied hard together and learned a lot about musicality . . . but being the age I was, my mind was naturally not always on the music.

There was one girl in particular who caught my fancy. Fight it as I may, I couldn't help but develop feelings for her. I didn't know what the heck to do with those feelings, so I asked some of my buddies what they thought I should do. The consensus was, since it wasn't too long until Valentine's Day, I should buy flowers and a card and ask her to the school dance.

It was, as they say, déjà vu all over again. My pals' advice hurled me back across time, through emotional distress, to the disastrous Valentine's Day swing-set episode with Mandy. But even though that grade-school wooing attempt had been scratched into my heart as a complete and utter failure, I was willing to risk history repeating itself and hope for a better outcome. *After all,* I figured, *I'm older now, accomplished in my music, and somewhat settled in my once-troubled soul. I can do this! I _need_ to do this!*

I mulled over my options for a week, and then I made my move.

HER NAME WAS HELEN, AND SHE WAS GORGEOUS. She had shoulder-length red hair, a face that would make anyone gaze in awe, and skin so perfect that it shone like expensive silk. Like Mandy from the fourth grade, Helen sat directly across from me in our little classroom "closet." But unlike Mandy, she wasn't the least bit shy; and when Helen spoke to me, she always smiled in such a way that I was convinced she liked me as much as I liked her.

On Valentine's Day I bought a big bouquet of red roses on my way to school. Once again, I made sure that I arrived in class before anyone else. I placed a card (store-bought this time) and the flowers down upon my intended's chair, and then I waited for everyone else to arrive.

The other four girls and Mrs. Gillan filed into the room and, as each one passed by Helen's chair, a little smile crossed their faces. They all knew that Helen didn't have a steady beau, and they were excited that she'd received flowers from someone. I acted completely nonchalant, intending to keep my status as a secret admirer safely intact until Helen opened the card. There was a new sensation bubbling up from within me that I can only describe as part delight and part terror.

A few minutes later, Helen entered the room. She picked up the bouquet, pressed it to her face, inhaled deeply, and smiled with her entire being as she opened the card. She appeared a little shocked as her eyes darted across the words, but then she put the flowers down and came over and gave me a big hug. It was the closest I'd been to a girl physically in years, and I was a little befuddled by the contact.

I couldn't judge the expression on Helen's face, but as she pulled away I thought I noticed the glimmer of a tear in her eye. Something told me this wasn't a tear of happiness, however; even though she thanked me again for the wonderful flowers, I had the feeling that something wasn't quite right. Sure enough, for the rest of the class Helen was not her usual carefree self, and I felt a wave of discomfort creep over me. I couldn't shake the feeling that perhaps I'd made a blunder—on Valentine's Day yet again!

After school, I dug up the nerve to call Helen to see what she had to say about "us." The news was just as I'd feared: She only wanted to be friends. She liked me very much, but she didn't feel "that way" about me and wasn't interested in pursuing a romantic relationship. As I hung up the phone, I could feel myself sinking into a fitful depression. How was it possible that I could have forgotten the lesson Mandy had beaten into me so many years before? Had I learned nothing about the folly of pursuing a girl on Valentine's Day? What the hell was I thinking?

I had the entire weekend to get my dejected spirit together again for Monday's class. Thankfully, seeing Helen wasn't as awkward as I'd imagined it would be. She was as sweet as pie to me, as if nothing uncomfortable had passed between us. I, however, needed a little time to fully regain my composure and recover from the humiliation I'd experienced. In fact, it took me several weeks to get my head together. But it could have been much worse if I hadn't had all sorts of other inner turmoil to occupy myself with.

I mean, with all of the questions I was still wrangling with about the Catholic faith, the existence of God, the purpose of life itself, and the difficulties I had to overcome trying to establish myself as a professional musician, Helen's rejection didn't really overwhelm me in the end. But it did add to a lingering depression that would follow me throughout high school, especially where girls were concerned.

I was playing music all the time and thriving with the Rain Dogs, but a part of me felt like it was missing. I needed more than mere social interaction; I wanted a girlfriend. Unfortunately, I wouldn't find a girl of my own until later on in my life. Patience has never been a strong suit of mine, but sometimes the universe teaches us that the more we hurry, the longer we end up having to wait for what we most want.

NOT LONG AFTER MY SECOND EMOTIONAL Valentine's Day massacre, the gifted music program expanded into two classes. Helen was moved into the other class, but Cathy joined our small group. Thank goodness I'm a slow learner when it comes to women because, even though I kept striking out, I kept going up to bat to try again.

I developed a huge crush on Cathy, as I had with Helen—and just like Helen, Cathy told me that she just wanted to be friends. Fortunately, this time I was smart enough not to broach the question of going steady, or even going on a date, on another Valentine's Day. I'd waited until the end of the school year to approach Cathy, which meant that when I was rejected, I didn't have to sit beside her for the rest of the semester. I'd also have the entire summer vacation to privately lick my wounds.

I thrust my energies back into music again and told myself to forget about girls and focus on being the best drummer I could be. I was still messing around with pot and booze (being in the world of jazz and rock 'n' roll, I was exposed to them both a lot), but I did my best not to fall too deeply into that hole. In fact, when it came to marijuana, I realized that I really didn't need it to fit in. I'd honestly never liked it that much anyway, often smoking it just because everyone else around me was. I'd been using pot for quite a while by this point, but I now made the decision to knock it off completely and forever. Music would be my drug of choice, and nothing would ever match the high I got from practicing hard or playing well.

My relationship with my parents was still on shaky ground when it came to school, but it *was* slowly improving. I now look back and thank God that I had my music to lead me through whatever darkness I encountered. Catholicism wasn't working for me anymore, and the large questions about life still rang incessantly in my mind. I continued to harbor a smoldering nugget of anger toward God that I'd been forced to grow up so different.

So many kids my age were concerned with looks and how they appeared, and I doubt they ever took a moment to place themselves in my shoes. I couldn't blame them for the things they thought were important. Even if what they valued seemed petty and shallow to me, who was I to judge? I'm sure they had their own doubts and were struggling to live up to who they thought they should be, or who others expected them to be. It was normal, really.

At a certain age I realized that I'd never be the same as any of them, ever. That's how I came to embrace a forward-moving life, using my music to pave the way. As I moved forward, I began to see that being burned had been a gift. If there really was a "road less traveled," then my accident had put me on that road.

♦ ♦ ♦

Chapter Eight

Higher Learning

They say that when a student is ready, the teacher appears. Soon I was to be both student *and* teacher.

After graduating from high school, I enrolled in Southeastern Louisiana University (SLU). It was about 30 miles from home, which meant that I could commute. I'd learned to drive by this point, which had given me much more freedom. I was now able to get to gigs on my own and could cruise around and have quiet time to think when life became too hectic.

I'd also been asked by the director of bands at SLU to audition for a scholarship. He didn't pass out such invitations often, but he did ask *me* to try out after visiting my high school near the end of my senior year.

The night before the audition, I was nervous. I was required to play a timpani piece; a snare-drum solo; and the marimba, which is similar to a xylophone. I'd never played the marimba before, so just prior to the audition I sight-read a short piece, figured out how to conquer the instrument, and nailed it at the performance.

A few weeks later, a letter arrived telling me that I'd been accepted and they were offering me a full scholarship! This was a great help since most of my income came from doing odd jobs at my dad's office, the occasional paying gig, and giving drum lessons at a nearby music store.

I hadn't been in a great frame of mind when I started giving these lessons. When I was onstage, I felt alive; away from my drums, I was still having trouble dealing with the hassles of everyday life, which would get my spirits down. But I've learned that to be a good teacher, you simply need to be open to the positive energy in the universe. In doing so, sometimes even the teacher becomes the student.

MY FRIEND RANDY OWNED A MUSIC STORE, and he asked if I'd like to get paid to teach some of his customers to play the drums. Needing the money, I figured, *What better job could there be than to teach people the thing I love most?*

Things were going along fine, until one morning when Randy called up to say he had a very special student for me. He requested that I come down right away, so I raced down to the shop. On my way inside, I practically tripped over a guy in a wheelchair who'd positioned himself in the middle of the doorway. I remember being annoyed that he was in my way and I had to squeeze around him to get inside to my student.

"Danny, I'm glad you're here," Randy said as I entered the shop. "I want you to meet your new student, Al. He's here for his first lesson."

I looked around the store but didn't see anyone except the irritating guy in the wheelchair. Turning back to Randy, I shrugged my shoulders and held out my arms, oblivious. "Where?"

"Right here. Danny, meet Al."

I looked down at the guy sitting limply in his wheelchair a few feet away. I nodded blankly in his direction, then put my arm on Randy's shoulder and steered him toward the back of the store. "Are you serious, man?" I whispered in his ear. "That guy is my student? You've gotta be kidding! What are you thinking?"

"You said you wanted to teach drums, didn't you?" Randy retorted, once we were out of Al's earshot. "Well, Al wants to learn to play drums. He's your student; you're his teacher. So go teach."

My next complaint echoed words I'd heard about myself a thousand times: "There's just no way . . . I can't teach the drums to somebody who barely sits up and drools all over himself. Just look at him! The guy's paralyzed!"

"What's the matter with you?" Randy asked in disbelief. "Don't you remember what it took for *you* to learn how to play? Do you think the world thought *you* would be a great drummer one day?"

I bit my tongue and put my ego in check, but maybe not enough. For some reason, I was angry that Randy would even think to ask me to teach drums to a person who probably couldn't hold the sticks much less beat out a tempo. Sighing heavily, I looked my friend right in the eye and said, "All right, I'll give it a shot. But if he doesn't respond, I'm done."

I wandered back over to Al, introduced myself, and vowed to make the best of it. I wheeled him to the far end of the store and into the practice studio where I'd set up two drum kits—one for the student, and one for me. I watched him as he sat in his chair admiring the set before him.

Al was a quadriplegic. On top of that, he wasn't able to talk—he had a computer with him that he typed on by moving a plastic stick along the keyboard with his chin, which would then "speak" whatever he'd typed in. Where the hell was I supposed to begin? The man couldn't sit in his chair without sliding toward the floor; the idea of him just holding a drumstick seemed out of the question.

Over the course of that first hour-long lesson, we didn't even try to play drums. Instead, we just got to know each other a little. I figured I had to know what had happened to him, what his ability was, and all that kind of stuff before I set up a game plan.

I asked questions, and Al typed his answers. Listening to the mechanical voice of his talking computer, he told me the following: he'd been in a car accident ten years before; he was left paralyzed below the neck, other than some slight use in his lower arms and left hand; he was unable to speak; and, moreover, he'd suffered severe head trauma that left him with the mental capacity of a ten-year-old. The more he told me, the more I thought, *Man, I better give this guy his money back. . . .*

But when our session was over and Al's nurse/ assistant arrived to pick him up, I asked her to bring him back again the next day. That's when I finally let him attempt to hold a drumstick. Al had been a guitar player before his accident, so he did have some musical sense buried deep inside his near-lifeless body. Maybe there was hope after all! (Or, I *hoped* there was hope.)

During that second session, Al was able to hold the stick with his left hand. But his grip was so weak that, as I watched him attempt to tap on the snare, I became immediately discouraged. I wanted to be a better teacher—wanted not to feel the way I was feeling—but I couldn't help myself. I was afraid that I couldn't help an individual with such severe limitations play an instrument again.

When Al left that second day, he hadn't made one solid drumbeat during our hour together. I went to talk to Randy. "I don't think I can do this. It's too much . . . the guy can hardly hold a stick. He can't do anything," I said flatly.

Boy, did Randy give it to me good when he heard that. "You're the most selfish person I have ever met," he shot back. "Don't you remember all the help and support you got when you began? You couldn't hold a stick in the beginning either—not for an entire month!"

That did it. I flew out of the store, jumped in my car, and burned rubber out of the parking lot. I went home and locked myself away with my drum set and played for hours, until every muscle in my body was aching and screaming for me to stop . . . and I kept going.

All the while I was thinking about Al, my own humble beginnings, and the world I'd carved out for myself on the music scene. Here I was, certainly not the picture of perfection, being judgmental about someone who I had more in common with than with many so-called able-bodied people. Had I so quickly forgotten my own struggles as a beginner and become so arrogant and ignorant?

I flopped down on my bed, exhausted and sweating, and looked up toward God or whatever force was out there in the universe. It was time to find my humility again, or I'd never be able to move on with my own growth—emotionally, professionally, or spiritually.

The next day I went to Randy and apologized for my behavior. I thanked him for pointing out the level of my selfishness and asked him to book Al for more lessons. In the coming months, I'd teach my student the same way I learned, figuring out how to hold the drumsticks in a way that would work for him.

I told Al that there wouldn't be any actual drumming at first. We were just going to focus on his life force, on finding a way for him to move the necessary fingers just enough to hold on to the stick—in other words, to accomplish something that most people would consider impossible. I knew that I just had to get Al to see the big picture, one tiny pixel at a time. If I could, then over the course of our lessons he'd finally find his way: he'd discover his own sound, his own tempo, and maybe even a new life. It was the least I could do—the *most* I could do!—to help a guy who just wanted to play the drums.

For months we barely made any progress, even though all I did was try to get him to focus on moving his fingers. We tried everything, eventually even employing some meditation techniques I'd taught myself. It might seem a bit loony, but tapping into all of the positive energy we could find really worked.

One morning, after spending four months trying to get a finger on Al's left hand to move, it began to twitch. At first I thought it was a spasm or something, but I could see in his eyes that Al felt it, and that he knew something momentous had just happened. He began to weep, and a surge of joyous energy ran up my spine and buzzed through my head.

Within a month or so, my student was holding a drumstick and even tapping the drumhead a few times. It was remarkable, but the drumming became secondary to what was really going on: a sort of spiritual healing that was transferring into this man's atrophied muscles and bones. By the end of the year, Al had defied all of the doctors who'd told him he'd never walk again—he had actually gotten up and was able to move around using a walker! Before long, he was even starting to speak. They may have only been monosyllabic words, but they were words nonetheless.

In the years to come, I'd often look back at Al's desire to play the drums despite the fact that so many others, including myself, had said it was impossible. He's the perfect example of the student teaching the teacher, and a testament to the power of positive thinking—something I was going to have to do a lot of myself in the months ahead.

ONE OF THE MOST FRUSTRATING walls of discrimination I'd face in my life was erected in the very place where personal freedom and open-mindedness are supposedly most encouraged—college.

Once I'd won my scholarship to Southeastern Louisiana University, I thought I was on my way. The depression that had dogged me since early high school lifted, partly because of winning the scholarship and partly because of the amazing transformation I was seeing in Al.

I was feeling good about myself, and my future was looking pretty sunny. But as I would learn, depression is a slippery animal that can disappear for a bit and then return to bite you in the butt when you're not looking.

I sure wasn't looking the day I showed up at SLU to register for the fall semester and finally met the jazz-band director. I'd been trying for weeks to contact him, since a major reason I was going to this college was to play in the jazz band, and I needed the director's written approval to join. Despite my repeated phone calls and e-mails, however, he wasn't responding to my messages.

My dad suggested that I just drive out to the campus to find this elusive director—the man who, temporarily at least, held my musical and academic future in his hands. I took his advice and knocked on the man's office door.

"Can I help you?" the director asked.

"My name is Dan Caro, sir. It's nice to meet you. I've been trying to contact you for weeks," I said, as politely as possible, as my eyes moved around the room admiring the fine music books and classic jazz posters lining the walls. "I'm a drummer, and I'll be attending classes here this fall. I'd like to get into the jazz band, so I was wondering if I could get your permission to do so."

He looked me in the eye, glanced down at where my hands should be, and brought his gaze back to my face. In that instant, I was certain that he knew exactly who I was—that he'd heard about "the burn boy" who wanted to get into the program. I knew in a second why all the messages I'd left for him had gone unanswered. In his eyes, I saw a look I'd seen hundreds of times before. It's the same look, I'm ashamed to admit, that I gave Al when I first met him—a look of prejudice.

Standing in this institute of higher learning, it didn't feel any different talking to a university professor than it had encountering a bully in the Terrytown school yard so many years before. I prepared myself for the blows to come. Even though I'd been on the receiving end of these since the age of two, it doesn't mean that it gets any easier to take the hit—just the opposite. It's like when my movie hero explains in *Rocky II* why he doesn't want to go back to fighting in the ring. He says that getting punched in the face 500 times a night stings after a while.

With sarcasm dripping from every word, the band director gave me the verbal version of a punch in the face: "How can *you* play drums?"

I kept my composure and patiently started to explain my technique to him. I'd brought a wristband and drumsticks in my bag to show him what I did, but he didn't allow me to demonstrate. Instead, he waved me toward the door. "We already have a drummer," he said. "And he's a grad student, not a freshman."

"But this is a state university, and I'm here on full scholarship," I protested. "I'm not asking for special treatment, I'm just asking to audition! The jazz band is supposed to be open for auditions to every student . . . I only want to—"

Cutting me off, the director repeated, "I said, we already have a drummer for the jazz band, and he's a grad student. You'll have to sign up for the improvisation-method class."

The improvisation-method class! That was a course in jazz basics, for God's sake! For beginners! At this stage in my career, I'd already played gigs with some top professionals. At the very least, I deserved to be allowed to audition; in fact, it was my academic right to be allowed to audition.

There's another scene from *Rocky II* that comes to mind when I meet people like this band director. Rocky's old trainer, Mickey Goldmill, warns our hero to be wary of the boxer he's about to step into the ring with, saying that the man doesn't just want to beat Rocky, he wants to humiliate him. (Please don't think that I live my life with a loop of *Rocky II* playing continually in my head, but there are definitely times when the story of the underdog being beaten down again and again resonates with me so intimately.)

I was furious with the jazz director and wanted to lash out, but there was nothing I could do. I had no power as a lowly freshman, and he was at the top of the academic pyramid. I couldn't even convince him to hear me play or take a minute of his time to let me show him how I could hold the drumsticks. But I wanted to play jazz, and this man was my key. There was only one other way to accomplish my goal.

"Improvisation method, eh?" I said, nodding my head, as I turned and left his office.

A few weeks later I was in my first "basics" class, and it was made up entirely of incoming freshmen with very little experience. I didn't want to appear overly confident with myself, but at the same time I didn't intend to purposefully hide the fact that I was already a professional musician.

I positioned myself behind my drum set and waited until it was time to jump in and show my mettle. Thirty minutes later, after all of the intro stuff and course-outline explanations, it was my turn to hit the skins. I started banging the hell out of those drums, and out of the corner of my eye, I could see the look of shock on the director's face. When I finished, the rest of the students applauded.

After class, as everyone else filed out the door, the director called me over for a private chat. "I'd like you to sit in on the jazz classes," he said. "I'd really like you in the band."

I guess I should have been flattered and elated. I'd proven myself and shown my ability. But the problem was that too much time had passed for me to be officially registered in his advanced class. It was impossible for me to drop the "basics" class now and enroll in the one he was asking me to "sit in" on. SLU had a strict policy on course selection: there was one week of add/drop, and that was it. After the first week, you were locked in to a schedule and no changes could be made. So, instead of being thrilled, I felt somewhat annoyed.

"You want me to sit in?" I repeated. "You do know that add/drop week is over, don't you?"

"Yes, I do. Just come and play. We could use you."

They could use me. Great! I wouldn't get any academic credit; it would be like playing a gig for free when everyone else in the band was getting paid. Half of me wanted to slug the guy, but my better half wanted to get my damn anger in check and do the thing I most wanted—play with that band. And if I'm going to be completely honest, I was hoping I'd get the chance to hear two little words from the man who was going to be my professor for the next semester. I wanted to hear him say, "I'm sorry."

I never heard those words.

In the end, it didn't matter if the band director apologized or not. The only thing his apology would have done was stroke my ego, and I was starting to realize how much my ego could hold me back. Instead, I accepted his offer to sit in, and I played with the jazz band without credit for the first year.

That year was amazing for me musically: I built up a solid reputation as a jazz drummer at the school, had a lot of fun, and was invited to be the lead drummer of the jazz band the following year.

But music and schoolwork made up just a part of my education that year. Thanks to my drumming student Al, who turned the tables of prejudice on me, I learned to look beyond my own ego and get to a place where I hoped I'd find peace of mind and maybe even happiness.

♦ ♦ ♦

Chapter Nine

In the Spirit

My musical career took off like a rocket at Southeastern Louisiana University, and I was suddenly finding myself in demand as a drummer. Not only was I playing with the three top academic bands at SLU, I was also gigging with at least three bands off campus. I found that I just couldn't say no when I was asked to perform, taking all the gigs that came my way. I was so busy some weeks that my classes became an afterthought.

More and more, I knew that music was where my heart was, and my heart was becoming lighter the more I played. That pesky depression I've talked about had finally begun to lift; in fact, most days I wouldn't even think about my personal problems. I was happy just practicing and playing music (and, when time allowed, studying).

But while my heart was often happy, my soul still craved answers. Since wandering away from Catholicism, I'd been searching for something to fulfill me spiritually. For a long while, I was certain that fulfillment could come solely from music. Yet as I ventured deeper into the world of the music industry, I began understanding what the word *industry* meant, and that I didn't exactly fit industry standards. It was a harsh lesson that began innocently enough while I was earning a little cash playing weddings and corporate parties with a jazz trio during my sophomore year.

At one of these events, we were approached by a woman who worked for a very large hotel/casino in Las Vegas. She came over and chatted the three of us up during our breaks and told us how much she liked our music. Before she left that night, she promised that she'd put in a good word for us with the entertainment promoter at the casino. Since he was a friend of hers, she told us there was an excellent chance he'd book us to play there.

I was excited, to say the least. I mean, I was just 19 years old and was almost assuredly on my way to play Vegas! A few weeks later, the casino promoter indeed called my bandmates and me and offered us an amazing gig. The deal was for a one-month booking at $2,000 per week, with all expenses paid. Not bad for a teenager!

We were faxed a contract and asked to send in a glossy photograph of the band that could be posted on the casino's marquee to promote our act. We didn't have a picture of us together as a group, but we were so excited to be asked for one that we rented tuxedos and hired a professional photographer to take our promo shots. We sent the pictures off to the promoter and waited to hear back regarding our travel arrangements. And we waited . . . and waited.

When the casino promoter finally called, I was given my first business lesson in big-time showbiz.

"Thanks for the photos," this guy said to one of my bandmates. "We still love your music and really want you guys to come out here and play, but we'll supply a drummer for you when you get here. Your drummer doesn't fit our image."

Until that moment, I'd naïvely believed that the music profession was about the music. How wrong I was! Once again I was being judged by how I looked, not by who I was or how well I played. It wouldn't have mattered if I'd been the greatest musician in the world; it seemed that the industry was all about looks and image. I cursed the casino, I cursed Las Vegas, and I cursed the words *business* and *industry.* I was so upset that I vowed never to pose for promotional photographs again—if a promoter or club manager ever insisted on a picture again, I'd hire a model to sit behind my drum kit for me.

The best part of this experience was that my bandmates refused to take the gig and go to Las Vegas without me. It was an act of friendship and loyalty I have never forgotten.

That Vegas rejection was like a wasp's sting, and the poison of it revived many of the old wounds I'd buried from years of insults and discrimination. As I kept discovering, though, it's impossible to bury past pain. What I'd eventually learn is that the only way to permanently deal with inner darkness is to open it up to the universe and let the light of positive energy shine on it.

But as a teen, I wasn't there yet. I still had demons dancing in my subconscious that pounced on any and every opportunity they could to resurface. So for a few months after the Vegas setback, the blues from my early teens made an unwelcome reappearance. Now, instead of being excited about landing gigs, I could only focus on being rejected, and I'm sure I sabotaged several musical prospects without even knowing it because of my negative energy.

WHEN I WORKED WITH AL at Randy's music store and dealt with the jazz director at SLU, I became aware of how energies—both positive and negative—could affect the creative impulse that drove the human spirit. Not long after the whole Vegas episode, I knew it was time to be done with any feelings of doubt and gloom. I was hungry to expand my world beyond the physical plane . . . I was ready to learn a better way. And because I was ready, because I was now a willing student, a teacher again appeared to me. One day I looked up, and there was Wolf.

His full name was "The Grey Wolf That Lives in the Corn That Not Even the Wind Can Touch," but his friends called him Grey Wolf, or just Wolf. He was married to a woman named Pale Moon, and the two of them were always in this coffee shop I liked to frequent. They were both Native American—she was Cherokee, and he was Choctaw. In fact, Wolf was once the leader of the Louisiana band of Choctaw Indians. He was also a Vietnam vet, a 25-year veteran of the local police department, and an incredibly well-rounded and in-depth man.

One day while I was waiting to get some coffee, Wolf nodded to me. Although we didn't speak to each other, I sensed an amazingly intense yet peaceful energy radiating from him, which I could feel from several feet away.

As I've mentioned, I'm pretty sensitive to the energy people give off, but I'd never encountered anything resembling the positive vibes I was picking up from Wolf. I was drawn to him right away and wanted to strike up a conversation, but I could see that he was busy chatting with his wife. Plus, I was running late for a rehearsal.

The band I was playing with at the time had a few out-of-town gigs, and several weeks passed before I went back to the coffee shop and saw Wolf again. This time he was sitting by himself, and his lovely wife was nowhere in sight. The memory of our brief encounter had stayed with me, so I went over and asked if I could sit with him while I drank my tea.

"Pull up a chair, my brother," he replied. His dark eyes were so deep and penetrating that it was if he were drawing me into his mind. He didn't even seem to notice my scars and instead looked right into my soul. When he talked to me, I felt that he was speaking to my heart, not my face.

"So tell me about yourself, Dan," he said as I took a seat across from him.

"You know my name?" I was surprised, as we'd never spoken before.

"Sure. I see you all the time, and it's kind of like family in here. I've asked about you from time to time, since I haven't seen you for a while. I was curious to meet you, but I didn't want to be intrusive, so I waited for you to come to me."

"Oh," I replied, surprised again. I told him that I was a musician and had been busy working, and I wondered why he'd been asking about me. "I'm sure you want to know what happened to me, right?"

Wolf looked me in the eye and said that while he was interested in what had happened to my body, what he really wanted to know was who I was as a spirit. *A spirit?* I'd never heard of anyone wanting to know about someone else's "spirit" before. The whole idea intrigued me. I knew that Wolf was Native American, but whatever limited information I had about his culture had been gathered from the movies or glossed-over history books— which is to say, I had no factual information whatsoever. My new friend was going to change all that.

As I told Wolf about my accident, I could feel his energy flowing through me, carrying me to a place in my mind I'd never explored before. He put me at ease while he brought out the deepest of my inner thoughts and beliefs, rough and jumbled as they may have been. He listened without judging, and he looked at me in the same way—he never averted his eyes from my face.

Later in the conversation, I asked about the spiritual element of his heritage. I knew I'd just stumbled upon something worthwhile, something that was now resonating loudly in my head and in my heart.

"Indians are spiritual in the sense that we have an appreciation and reverence for our environment," Wolf explained. "We give thanks for being alive, and we thank the 'Great Spirit' for providing us with food and shelter. The Earth has a spirit that she shares with us, so we are grateful for that."

I was quite intrigued by what Wolf said. During our many talks about spirituality over the years, I came to learn that most religions have the same core belief system and are more or less aligned with each other. Except for terminology and ritual, there isn't a great deal of difference between the heart of Christianity and the spiritual wind of the Choctaw—a great spirit drives and inhabits us all. When I discovered that, my mind opened up like a spigot, and all of these amazing thoughts and feelings began flowing through me. My spiritual self was awakening, and I saw my life in a new light. This light was so intense that my self-doubts, insecurities, and depression could no longer find a place to hide.

Wolf was what you might call my first guru. He taught me new ways to look at the world and, in many ways, helped me liberate my spirit.

IN MY NEWFOUND FREEDOM, I found the courage to once again open myself up to a young lady.

I met Ariel at a café near the SLU campus. I was settling into one of its coveted window seats when I noticed an exotic-looking girl across the street. I was daydreaming about what it would be like to meet such an attractive woman when she ran across the road, came inside, and started chatting with the people at the table next to mine. A couple minutes later she was somehow sitting across from me and asking me about music.

"My friends tell me that you're a musician and your name is Dan. So, Dan," she said with a big smile, "all day I've been trying to figure out who sings the song 'Cat's in the Cradle.' Any idea?"

I was flustered by both her openness and the way she was so immediately at ease with me. I managed to respond, "Harry Chapin, I think." Although I was trying my hardest to sound calm and cool, I knew that I must be coming across as a little nervous. Yet within a couple minutes, I realized there was absolutely no need for me to be nervous around this girl.

Ariel was an SLU student as well, and different from any woman I'd ever met. She was sweet, funny, and easygoing; and she made me feel right at home in her company. In some ways, she reminded me of my friend Matt from high school, a person with no pretensions who just wanted to be friends with me for friendship's sake.

Ariel and I spent the entire afternoon together discussing the music of the '60s, life at SLU, what we wanted to accomplish in our lives, and a thousand other topics that young people who really like each other talk about just so they don't have to say good-bye.

We became good friends, and pretty soon we were inseparable. Our romance blossomed, and it was everything I'd hoped my first relationship would be. I often thought about those long, lonely nights I'd spent in my room convinced that I'd never find anybody. It amazed me how a seemingly simple shift in attitude (from negative to positive, which I'd made with Wolf's help) could make such a profound difference in a person's life. As my parents would say, I was "over the moon in love," and it was definitely worth the wait.

ARIEL AND I REGULARLY ENDED UP at the home of her best friend, Linda, whose family was fairly wealthy. What I learned during those visits was that money truly can't buy happiness, nor does it make someone a good or decent person. These are all lessons I learned thanks to Linda's dad.

On one particular afternoon, Ariel and I were chatting with Linda and her stepmom in their kitchen. The four of us were having a great conversation, but it was hard for us to hear each other over the loud voices and raucous laughter coming from the adjoining room. Linda said that her dad and one of his buddies were having a few drinks and settling in to watch a football game.

We all decided to head in and join them, and Linda's stepmother introduced me to her husband and his pal. The two were holding Scotch glasses that were filled to the brim, and they were clearly feeling no pain. As soon as I was introduced, the friend leered at Ariel and then leaned over to Linda's dad. In an obnoxiously loud voice, he blurted out: "Look at that dude. I can't believe such a cute girl is hooked up with that! I wonder if he's even got a dick!"

"Yeah," the father agreed with a laugh. "He's probably dickless! She could do a lot better than that!"

Everyone in the room heard what these two "gentlemen" had to say about me. Linda's stepmom, who was a genuine lady, tried to change the subject and cover up her husband's vulgar faux pas by acting overly sweet. She was clearly embarrassed and angry that a guest had been verbally assaulted in her home. Ariel took hold of my arm and squeezed it affectionately. Linda ushered us out of the room and out of the house, apologizing profusely for the rude behavior of her father and his friend. But I cut her short, telling her she had nothing to apologize for. *She* hadn't been the shallow one, the intentionally stupid and tactless one.

The truly strange and wonderful thing about the entire incident was that I wasn't even bothered by the horrible thing those two louts said about me in front of my girlfriend.

A few months earlier, I would have been devastated by such public humiliation and probably would have locked myself in the house and beaten my drums mercilessly for weeks. But ever since I'd met Wolf, and then Ariel, my entire outlook on life had changed. I was on a quest to be a better, more enlightened person, one who was more concerned with being happy than harboring grudges. When I told Linda not to worry about what happened because it didn't matter, I meant it—it didn't matter at all.

Ariel and I dated on and off for a few years. She really did bring out a side of me that I thought would never come to light, and I remain thankful to her for that. When we eventually broke up, it seemed like the right and natural thing to do. There was no fighting, no rancor, and no animosity. Rather, there was a mutual understanding that we needed to move apart. We remain friends, though, and are still there for each other to this day if one needs the other.

Sadly, Wolf died just before my 22nd birthday. He was very ill and drifted in and out of consciousness near the end, but I was fortunate enough to have been by his bedside and hold his hand not long before he passed over. He was a true friend and a wonderful teacher, and I greatly miss him and our talks. But I know that he's rejoined the Great Spirit that surrounds us all—the Spirit that he introduced me to—and that his eternal journey toward the Divine continues. Wolf turned my own spirit toward infinity, and before he left this world, I'd already taken my first steps toward fulfilling my destiny.

◆ ◆ ◆

Chapter Ten

Living the Dream

My friend and spiritual mentor, Wolf, had opened my eyes to the wonder of an all-connected universe and inspired me to begin a journey toward enlightenment. Although I'd once thrived at SLU, the school now felt too small for me. After two years, I felt that I'd learned everything I could there, so it was time to move onward and upward.

My new path began at the doors of Loyola University in New Orleans. The school was a perfect fit for me, as it had one of the best music programs in the entire country, if not the world. In addition to its excellent music department, Loyola is also renowned for its humanity courses, and I was hungry to learn as much as I could. In the end, I decided to major in music therapy—but I also signed up for electives in philosophy, psychology, Eastern religions, and political theory.

Things got off to a rocky start, however. I was determined to play in the school's famed varsity jazz ensemble, one of the finest college bands in America, but I was absolutely stymied by their "blind audition" process. It's called that because while the students could watch each other audition, the judges sat behind a temporary wall and could only *hear* the audition pieces, supposedly unaware of who was playing.

I thought that it wasn't going to be very hard for the judges to figure out which student was playing at any given time, since we each had our own unique style. Also, I was the only left-handed drummer in the school, which meant that I had to change the position of the drum kit before I played. I just assumed this would tip the judges off to my identity.

My performance was one of the best I've ever given, and I was sure that it was better than what the other students had done. I was 100 percent certain I'd made the cut, but I didn't. Instead, I was relegated to play with the junior jazz ensemble. At the time I thought nepotism was to blame, because the son of one of the judges was among the small group auditioning for the ensemble. I realize now that it was just my ego getting in the way—and, looking back, maybe I just wasn't as great as I thought I was!

I was furious when I received the news that I hadn't made the ensemble, once again feeling the bitter bite of discrimination. But at least instead of moping about it or filing an official complaint, I channeled my disappointment and frustration into something creative and positive. I was determined to be gracious about being passed over, whatever the reason had been. I'd now concentrate on doing what I loved best.

So that year I played my heart out for the junior jazz ensemble and was grateful for the experience. In the meantime, I spent every night and weekend preparing for my next audition for the varsity jazz ensemble, which would come the following year. And you guessed it— I nailed it! I was even chosen as one of the two principal drummers of the ensemble and invited to perform at universities and concert halls throughout the United States.

I never would have been given this incredible opportunity had I not made the decision to stay upbeat after my failed audition attempt. I was learning to be more positive in all kinds of so-called negative situations. My mind and heart were opening up to the universe, and it was responding in kind: the more open I was, the more good things came my way.

AT LOYOLA, I MET ALL SORTS OF INCREDIBLE PEOPLE. Perhaps the most incredible of them all was Johnny Vidacovich, known to his friends and fans in the Big Easy simply as "Johnny V."

Johnny V is, without exaggeration, one of the greatest drummers in the world. He's played with the best musicians on the planet, such as John Scofield; Professor Longhair; Stanton Moore; Charlie Hunter; Willy DeVille; George Porter, Jr.; and Dr. John, to name a few. He's a permanent fixture on the New Orleans jazz scene and a living legend in the music industry. He's also eccentric, funny, insightful, amazingly well read, and brilliant. As you can probably tell, I like Johnny immensely and consider him one of my great and true friends.

Although I'd known about Johnny for years through his music, I first met him at Loyola, where he was one of my drumming instructors. But he wasn't just an instructor. Like Wolf, he was a *teacher* in the truest sense of the word, teaching me as much about life (if not more) as about playing drums.

Johnny had a house in Mid-City New Orleans, and he invited me there for my first one-on-one class. Within minutes of arriving at his place, I knew I wasn't going to be in for a standard music lesson. I don't even think he said hello to me before asking one of those deep, soul-searching questions about life that people usually spend years sitting on a Tibetan mountaintop trying to figure out how to answer.

The first thing he said to me was: "Who are you, Dan? Tell me who Dan Caro really is." I had no idea what he was asking, or how I should answer. I just looked at the drumsticks I was carrying and then back at him.

"Okay, let's start there," he continued, following my gaze. "Can those sticks speak for you? Is who you are as a person obvious by the way you play your music? What I'm asking you is this: can you tell me your life story through your drums?"

"I have no idea," I replied, taken aback by his offbeat teaching method.

"Well, the first thing we need to find out is who 'Dan' is, in order for you to move beyond where you are now. You might sound like Buddy Rich or some other superfamous drummer, but your music won't mean a thing until you can tell people who you are with those drumsticks you're holding."

I don't remember if a smile crossed my face, but I was sure smiling inside. I thought, *Man, studying with this guy is going to be one hell of a trip!*

And what a trip it was! Johnny was keenly interested in a drummer's individuality, along with the landscape of a musician's "inner life." He had no intention of teaching me technique; he was going to teach the "philosophy" of drumming rather than the mechanics of it.

One day, Johnny decided that we should play together on two drum kits that were facing each other in the center of the room. He put on a CD of one of Bach's *Brandenburg Concertos* and told me to play without stopping. After I reminded my teacher that Bach hadn't written music for a jazz drum, nor had there been any drum kits kicking around Europe in the 1700s, he told me to stop thinking and just play.

As I hit the skins, Johnny began shouting out suggestions: "Play it with a rock beat, but don't play the rock pattern! Toss in the jazz beat . . . now go back and make it rock! Make it *new* rock 'n' roll!" Suggestion after crazy suggestion flew at me, as my sticks danced across the drumheads and cymbals so quickly that my mind couldn't keep up with what I was doing. I was playing as hard I could, and Johnny yelled, "Don't play on the drum skins, man, play on the rims! Play on the drum stand!"

I shifted my focus and changed the amount of force I was using and the way I used my sticks. I didn't know *what* this guy wanted, but I knew I was out of my comfort zone. It was like barreling headlong down the highway in a car doing 80 miles per hour and then

suddenly being told to drive in reverse and pop a whee-
lie at the same time. My mind was awhirl and my sticks
were flying.

"Good, good, don't think! Be in the moment!" Johnny
shouted over the banging. "Play the soul of the drums,
the spirit of the drums!" I was aware of him playing on
the kit opposite me, but I wasn't paying attention to
much else going on around me. I was feeling my environment instinctively, somehow just picking up on what he
was playing.

A moment later, without talking about it, Johnny and
I had synched up perfectly. I remember one instant when
we played the exact same groove, in the exact same way,
at the exact same time. And at the risk of sounding overly
dramatic, it was beautiful. I felt as if I were floating above
my body and time was standing still.

He and I continued to play, synching up with each
other and then moving away, back and forth, back and
forth—as if we were speaking to each other through our
instruments. I was telling him the story of who I was with
my drums, and he was responding. Neither of us stopped
to discuss it; we just kept going until we couldn't play
anymore.

Even though I was exhausted, I couldn't help but mention the perfect interaction we'd created playing together.
Johnny told me that we'd tapped into the constant flow
of energy that eternally passes through the universe, an
energy that connects us all together, which we can tap
into if we just open ourselves up to the Divine.

"You see, when you let go, magic happens," my new
teacher explained.

That did it for me. My mind started to tingle, and a million questions flooded my brain. I wanted to know everything Johnny knew, and I wanted to know it right away. I started asking him question after question about what he meant. Laughing, he held up his hand and said, "Danny, you have to relax. It will come to you when it comes to you. Until you're ready to open up, you'll never hear the answers. And all the answers come from within anyway, not from without."

IN TIME, JOHNNY V BECAME my biggest spiritual influence. Just as I had with Wolf, I spent hours hanging out with Johnny discussing religion, philosophy, and spirituality. We talked about how to remain in touch with our creative spirit in everyday life, as well as how to remain open to the positive energies of the universe and channel them through our music and art—as he'd showed me during our Bach experience.

We also explored concepts I was learning about in my humanities courses at Loyola, such as what the ego was and what it could do. I was learning how it affected the way I communicated with other people, with myself, and with the universe.

Up until this point, I'd never once thought that I had an ego, which I'd assumed was a three-letter word for an excess of personal pride and arrogance. Now I understood that the ego is actually a blinded sense of self that can act like a spiritual anchor by fastening any of us to petty concerns and blocking our creative force.

Ironically, Johnny and I rarely discussed drumming itself! Instead, he introduced me to new rhythms of thoughts and ideas. He also loaned me some groundbreaking and thought-provoking books—including

The Celestine Prophecy by James Redfield, *Sophie's World* by Jostein Gaarder, and *Be Here Now* by Ram Dass— which opened my mind. And by opening my mind, they opened up my drumming, too.

Johnny V taught me to allow inspiration to flow through me and out of my drumsticks. And when I just relaxed and let go, as he told me to do, the "magic" happened. Soon I was playing better than ever and getting gigs all over New Orleans, including at some of the oldest and most famous jazz clubs in the world.

With this new confidence surging through me, I decided to branch out musically with fellow Loyola student Brandon Tarricone, who was an excellent guitarist. Brandon and I began jamming together, and our sound was so good that we recruited a few other musicians to form a band. Calling ourselves the "Brotherhood of Groove," we had a terrific, funky sound. Soon we had more bookings than we could handle, on campuses and in clubs around New Orleans. We were all still just students and were amazed by how quickly our band took off. In fact, our success was a bit of a "problem" when it came to school because our rigorous booking schedule conflicted with our classes and assignments. But we were loving it all so much that there was no way we were going to stop.

SIX MONTHS AFTER THE BAND WAS FORMED, we booked time at the best recording studio in New Orleans, hired some top-ranked session musicians to fill out our sound, and started working on our first CD. We spent a month laying down tracks and perfecting the mix for the final recording. It was a mind-blowing experience. Not only were we in a successful band, but we were in control of our musical careers as well.

I'd sure come a long way from that 12-year-old boy who struggled to figure out a way to hold on to a drumstick. Now in my early 20s, I was a professional musician earning a living from my music. In many ways, I'd made it—I was living the dream!

The first run for our CD was more than a thousand copies, and they sold like hotcakes. Since we didn't have an agent, Brandon and I spent our "spare" time lining up even more gigs and marketing the sound of the Brotherhood of Groove. I handled the promotion while Brandon booked the gigs. We managed to do a pretty good job; in fact, the band grew so successful that we had to take the next big step.

For so many years as a student, my schoolwork had suffered because my heart was in my music, and that's where I'd put my time and dedication. So it made sense to me at this point to make a choice and go all the way with it. After my second year at Loyola, I left school to play full-time.

Before I knew it, the Brotherhood of Groove was moving beyond the Big Easy and taking our show on the road. We toured all over the country, which was a fantastic experience. I got to visit cities I'd only seen in movies, and play in clubs I'd only read about in trade magazines and newspapers. But touring also taught me that living this kind of dream routinely meant going with little or no sleep, spending weeks in cramped vans with cranky musicians, eating fast food three times day, and being so homesick it hurt. Like anything, the dream had its ups and downs, but we all went with the flow.

During one tour, the band ended up in Philadelphia, where we were booked to perform in a small place called "Dr. Watson's Pub" (also known as just "Doc Watson's"), an old club with a 1950s feel and decor. The gig was a disaster because the owner had double-booked us with another band, and he tossed us out on our ears without paying us a penny.

Yet one great thing happened on this trip: we drove past the Philadelphia Museum of Art. Although my bandmates were exhausted, they knew what a huge fan I was of Rocky Balboa. They were good enough to pull over to the curb and told me to go for it.

The numerous steps leading up to the museum are, of course, the ones that Rocky struggles with at the beginning of his training for the big fight. Later on, lean and pumped up, he runs up those same steps and does a victory dance at the top, arms and fists held high. The guys were right—I had to do it! So while they waited in the car, I went out into the cold Philadelphia night. I ran all the way to the top of the steps, which seemed symbolic of the obstacles I'd overcome, and pumped my own arms in victory.

Then I headed down, back to the band waiting in the car . . . and toward what lay ahead.

IN 2002, AFTER TWO YEARS AND 350 EXHAUSTING GIGS in more cities than I can remember, I figured that the road had taught me everything it could. I'd had enough of the grueling tour schedule and told the band I was going to leave as soon as they could find another drummer. Once they did, I decided to take a few months off to refuel my spirit, catch my breath, and do some reading.

The break renewed my energy, even though I was a little nervous that I'd go broke and people would forget me if I hung low for a bit. But I wasn't *that* worried. With my new in-touch-with-the-universe philosophy, I'd learned to trust that it would provide, and that my talents were going to lead me into my new life as a freelance musician.

My trust was well founded. My phone began ringing off the hook as soon as word circulated around New Orleans that I'd left the Brotherhood of Grove and was now a free agent. It wasn't long before I was playing regular gigs with Michael Ray & the Cosmic Krewe. Michael is a legendary trumpet player who's toured and performed with Kool & the Gang for nearly 20 years, among many other musical milestones. So whenever Michael was in New Orleans, I'd play with the Cosmic Krewe; whenever he was away with Kool & the Gang, I was free to play with other bands all over New Orleans. It was a perfect setup for me, professionally and creatively.

On any given night, I could be playing with a band I'd never played with before, mastering a repertoire I'd never attempted. Life as a freelancer was making me a better performer *and* a better musician, and for the next few years my career blossomed as it never had before. It was a challenge, but luckily, I was used to challenges.

But the biggest challenge I have ever faced—and probably the biggest challenge anyone living in New Orleans was *ever* to face—was taking shape somewhere over the Bahamas. It was late August 2005, and something devastating was about to sweep through all of our lives.

Her name was Katrina.

◆ ◆ ◆

Chapter Eleven

The Winds of Change

In the summer of 2005, I was at the top of my game professionally. I was performing regularly with a dozen different bands and filling in as a substitute drummer for several others. I had recorded with some of the best players in the industry and had established my reputation as a solid jazz musician in the birthplace of jazz itself. My music was maturing, and I felt that I was at my peak.

The rest of my life was falling nicely into place as well: I'd purchased my own home just outside of New Orleans in Metairie, I'd made some great friends, my family was healthy, and I'd even adopted a great little mutt of a dog named Dixie. Life was good.

And then Hurricane Katrina hit and blew my world—and the city I loved—into a million shattered pieces.

LIKE MOST OF US WHO CALLED southeastern Louisiana our home, I had no idea what was coming at us from across the Gulf of Mexico. I'd seen plenty of big storms before, and of course the Big Easy had weathered more than its share of hurricanes. Yet no one was expecting the mega-killer that smacked into Louisiana on Monday, August 29, leaving more than 1,800 people dead and destroying much of the Gulf Coast, from Florida right across to Texas.

At first, Katrina seemed as if it was going to be like any other bad tropical storm. Then when it was upgraded to a hurricane, it was only a category 1, which is the lowest level of hurricane classification. This is really nothing to be afraid of, even when you live in a city that's below sea level (like New Orleans). Nevertheless, something about Katrina bothered me from the start.

Well before officials told people to evacuate, I decided to get out of town until the storm blew over. On Saturday, August 27, I called up my old high-school buddy Matt Rycyk, who'd moved to Atlanta a couple of years previously. Matt and I had remained close, and I had even been asked to stand up for him at his wedding. When he got on the phone now, it was obvious that he'd heard about the hurricane. Before I had a chance to say anything other than hello, he and his wife invited me to come to Georgia and stay with them for as long as I wanted.

Since there was no great urgency to leave, I took my time wandering around my house. As I tried to figure out what to take with me, I realized that I'd become detached from everything I owned. They were just belongings, not what made *me* belong. I ultimately grabbed a change of clothes, put some bottled water and a couple of cans of food in a bag, and jumped into the car with Dixie to begin the 500-mile drive to Atlanta. That evening, I was sitting with Matt and his wife in their living room talking about old times. None of us had any idea that while we were reminiscing, Katrina was morphing into a superstorm over the warm waters of the Gulf of Mexico.

When I woke up the next morning—still 24 hours before it smashed into New Orleans—I found out that Katrina had been labeled a category 5 hurricane, which is as bad as it gets. It was a monster, and it was moving toward my hometown at 175 miles per hour. I got a sick feeling deep in my gut that New Orleans was doomed. Luckily, I'd spoken to my parents before I left for Georgia, and I knew they were going to stay at my brother Johnny's house in New Iberia, a safe 150 miles west of New Orleans. I was glued to Matt's television, waiting to see what would happen.

When it hit New Orleans on the morning of August 29, Katrina devastated the city. I watched the TV news in horror as the tragedy unfolded—the swamped neighborhoods, the unimaginable human pain and suffering . . . so many terrible images. And things just got worse. It was impossible to reach anyone in New Orleans by phone, but luckily I could communicate with my family by text messaging. I thanked God that they were all safe.

I had to stay in Atlanta for two weeks before I could finally get back to Louisiana and reunite with my family. We stayed together at Johnny's place in New Iberia for two months, waiting and watching as the floodwater slowly receded.

Eventually, folks were allowed to visit their abandoned homes. I was lucky in that my house in Metairie was far enough west of New Orleans not to have been flooded. However, there weren't any basic services available, such as power or fresh water. The entire region was in chaos, a total mess.

New Orleans would eventually dry out, but it was left in ruins. The entertainment business, for instance, had been completely wiped out; for the first time in centuries, the music of the Big Easy was silenced. Since the heart and soul of the city were gone, I decided to leave as well. What else could I do? I earned my living playing music, and virtually every musician I knew was either homeless or unemployed (or both)! My musical career in New Orleans was over for the foreseeable future, and I had to go somewhere else. But where? Where could I go and earn a living with a pair of drumsticks?

I looked north and set my sights on New York City. *After all,* I thought, *I know a few people there, and the city does have some of the world's most renowned jazz clubs.*

My parents didn't want me to move—especially my dad, who thought that the competition among drummers in New York would be brutal and the music scene impossible to break into. While I appreciated his concern, I wasn't going to change my mind. I needed a change, and New York was it.

I RENTED A U-HAUL AND LOADED UP MY DRUMS and a few furnishings. So many family friends had been displaced by Katrina that I didn't even think about renting my house out. I just let whoever needed a place go ahead and use it.

Dixie and I hit the road, leisurely zigzagging our way through the scenic countryside to our new life. I found an apartment that allowed dogs (but not drums, so I had to be sneaky) in the Bay Ridge section of Brooklyn, not far from the foot of the amazingly long and beautiful Verrazano-Narrows Bridge.

New York was a whole new world and a completely different lifestyle, a huge metropolis where very few people gawked at me . . . or even noticed my appearance, for that matter. One of the great things about New Yorkers is that they're not shocked by anything "different"; rather, the city embraces differences. Walking through my new neighborhood was like walking through the United Nations—it was filled with Russians, Indians, Muslims, and Polish people. I was the minority, and not because I looked physically different. It was refreshing and liberating to go to the store and never be pointed at or laughed at, no matter how crowded the streets were.

At night I'd take the subway across the East River into Manhattan. When I could afford it, I'd hang out at some of the city's most famous jazz clubs, like the Village Vanguard, Birdland, Iridium, and the Blue Note. I became a frequent patron of several other clubs, and I began sitting in with different bands and even scoring a few of my own gigs. It was an incredibly exciting time. Even though it would be tough, I knew I'd be able to carve out a living in New York if I wanted.

What's interesting is that I wasn't as obsessed with professional success as I had been earlier in my life. First of all, I didn't have a need to prove myself on that level anymore—I knew what I was capable of and wasn't looking for validation. But more important, Katrina had changed me. I was increasingly asking myself what my purpose was in this short time on Earth we're all allotted. I'd worked so hard to reach the pinnacle of musical success in New Orleans, and then overnight a wind had come dancing across the water and taken it all away from me. In the end, what did my success matter? What difference did it make to anyone in this world other than me?

There was something stirring deep within me, and I knew that I was transitioning to a new phase of my life. I took long walks along the waterfront and looked out over the harbor toward the Statue of Liberty, or across the river at the cosmopolitan beauty of the Manhattan skyline. The enormity of New York gave me an unfamiliar sense of anonymity and a great deal of time to be alone with my thoughts.

I was able to do a lot of soul-searching during this time, spending many hours reflecting on the journey I'd begun on March 17, 1982, the day I was burned. Looking back at where I'd come from—all that I'd suffered through and accomplished—I realized that the only thing I truly owned was my unique life experience. I thought I could help others by sharing it . . . so I decided that's what I'd do next.

I was excited by the thought of telling my story to as many people as I could. Hopefully, I'd help someone else struggling with the type of challenges I'd dealt with most of my life—and perhaps I'd even be able to inspire others. Yet I had no idea how to get my story out into the world. Helping people had been my motivation when I agreed to appear on *The Montel Williams Show* more than a decade earlier, a show that had reached millions of viewers. But it wasn't as though television producers were currently calling me up trying to book me as a guest.

I told myself that maybe one day I would get that call. And if playing the drums had taught me anything, it was to practice and be ready when opportunity knocked. So I resolved to learn how to best tell my story and be ready for the day when someone asked to hear it.

I enrolled in a workshop taught by a hugely successful public speaker and author named Steve Siebold. Talk about inspiring! After one good conversation, he told me that I should become an inspirational speaker. "Start telling your story," he advised. "People will listen."

Steve was patient with me and taught me how to get to the core of what I had to say. After a few meetings, he even offered me the position of president at a local speaking club he was forming in New York City. I was hugely flattered, but I didn't think I was ready for that kind of responsibility. I told him that I'd just keep studying the tips he'd given me. I was certain my life was changing direction, and I wanted to learn as much about public speaking as I could. More and more I was feeling the call to pass along my message of how to live life positively, no matter what the hardships were.

It was around this time that I began thinking seriously about becoming a Shriner. This seemed like one of the best ways I could give back and repay that amazing group of people who'd taken such good care of me all those years ago. Without the Shriners, I would have died at Charity Hospital in New Orleans within a few days of my accident. Without question, they'd saved my life.

The Shriners do a lot of good for people, but they're mostly known for coming to the aid of kids who are hurt, suffering, and in desperate need of help. They did that for me, and I wanted to help them keep doing it for others. As it turned out, I'd soon get some firsthand experience helping others in need, experience that hit very close to home.

THE CALL CAME LATE ONE NIGHT while I was reading in my Brooklyn apartment, and it was the kind of call no one ever wants to receive.

When I picked up the phone, I heard the shaky and troubled voice of my father, who is not the kind of man who lets his emotions carry him away. "Danny, it's your brother Paul," he said. "He's sick and needs help. Can you come home right away?"

"What is it, Dad? What's wrong with Paul?"

"I can't believe it, but it's drugs . . . heroin. He's hooked. Your mom and I are so worried, and we just don't know what to do."

I tried to calm my dad down and find out what was going on with my kid brother. It turned out that Paul was another victim of Katrina—the death and devastation he'd witnessed had hit him hard, and he'd turned to hard drugs to cope. He'd been living at home, but then he drifted away from the family after the storm's devastating aftermath. My parents had done their best to make my brother happy and keep him healthy, but they couldn't get him off drugs. Mom and Dad had tried to reason with him, but the dope had a very strong hold on Paul.

I knew there was no reasoning with an addict, but I also knew I had to get home to be with my little brother.

"Don't worry, Dad," I said, knowing how much my parents loved their sons and how freaked out they must be. "Paul's a good kid, and he's going to be fine. Tell Mom not to worry . . . I'll be home by supper tomorrow, and everything's going to be okay."

The truth was that I was worried sick about Paul. I knew he was a sensitive kid, and I could only imagine how shaken up he must have been in the wake of Katrina.

When I hung up after talking with my dad, it was nearly midnight, and I spent the rest of the night booking an early-morning flight and arranging for a friend to take care of Dixie. Soon after sunrise, I was in the air and headed back home, back to what was left of New Orleans and to my troubled family.

I didn't know exactly what to expect after talking to my father; I just knew I was scared. But when I got home and knocked on the guest-room door, my worst fears evaporated. Paul's face lit up like a thousand-watt bulb as soon as he saw me, and I knew he was going to be all right. Of course, it was going to take a lot of work and a lot of love, but that's exactly what I came to give.

I didn't leave my brother's side for the next two weeks. I took him to AA meetings three times a day, for walks outside in the park to reconnect with nature, and to play basketball and go bowling. I wanted him to see what I'd learned over the years: that negative energy can be rerouted into positive activities that are physically healthy and emotionally fulfilling.

Paul and I would talk late into the night about philosophy and spirituality because I wanted him to begin his own spiritual journey—one that was guided by light, not haunted by the darkness of drug abuse. I opened up to him about my own struggles, as well as the way Johnny V and Wolf had helped me come to understand my spirit and awaken the best parts of me.

A couple weeks later, Paul was looking much better, so I brought him to New York for a change of scenery. I hoped that the city would be invigorating and rejuvenating for him; indeed, not long after we arrived, I could see him beginning to flourish, which made my parents ecstatic. Still, drug addiction is a serious problem, and I knew that my brother was going to need professional help to beat it permanently. A friend of mine who was a former cocaine addict suggested I take Paul to a very good rehabilitation facility in Georgia that my buddy knew about. We discussed it, and my brother agreed to go in order to put the cap on his own recovery.

TWO YEARS AFTER KATRINA HIT, I decided to head back to Louisiana so I could be there for Paul when he returned from rehab. I promised my brother that I'd always be there for him, and it was a promise I was going to keep.

Today, Paul is clean and sober and thriving in a new career, and our bond is even stronger now than it was before. I'm honored that he let me help him deal with his challenges, and I hope he knows how much *he* helped *me*. Thanks to him, I knew for certain that it was time to start focusing my energies on helping others. Among other things, I did decide to become a Shriner. So when Mike Andrews, the executive vice president of Shriners International, called a few months later and asked me to become one of their ambassadors, my answer was an emphatic *yes!*

The first time I'd spoken to Mike was back in 2003. He'd called me at home in New Orleans and asked if I'd be willing to be featured in a short documentary titled *Without Limits,* which would promote the good works of the Shriners Hospitals for Children. The filmmakers wanted to chronicle how the Shriners had helped me survive and, through countless surgeries, made it possible for me to live a relatively normal and successful life.

Mike told me that the film would premiere at the Shriners International convention in Minneapolis that summer, and he asked if I'd speak to the audience and play the drums for them. I happily agreed to it all, telling Mike that it would be an honor to help in any way I could.

A few weeks later, the film crew arrived at my home and spent several days shooting footage of my family and me. They even followed me to some of my gigs and filmed me playing like a madman at a jazz club in New Orleans. That July, the Shriners flew my parents and me to Minneapolis, and we watched the debut of *Without Limits* with thousands of Shriners from all over the world.

As promised, I went onstage after the screening and began playing the drums. It turns out that I had to play louder than I'd ever done in any club—because in the middle of my brief set, I received the largest standing ovation of my life. After I finished, I gave a short talk about my journey from burn victim to professional musician, all thanks to the Shriners.

Later, Mike told me he thought I'd done so well that I should consider a career as an inspirational speaker. While I shrugged off his suggestion at that point, Mike planted a seed in my head that ended up blossoming a few years later when I was in Brooklyn, looking for a new direction after Hurricane Katrina.

MY FATHER HAD HEARD Mike's suggestion at the convention in 2003. He agreed that I'd be a good speaker, if only I could overcome my debilitating shyness. So, that same year, I joined the New Orleans chapter of Toastmasters International, a worldwide group that helps members improve their public-speaking skills. In essence, they teach you how to speak in front of large groups of people and not be scared to death!

I tagged along with Dad to a series of meetings, but at first I was too timid to speak. I wore dark, baggy clothes to try to hide myself; and when I was called upon to give a presentation, I'd tense up and my heart would pound so hard I thought my ribs would break. And when I tried to talk about being burned and the challenges I'd faced, I'd get too emotional. Instead, I'd hook up a VCR and pop in the *Without Limits* video and let that tell the hard parts. When the movie was over, I'd talk about learning to play drums and then let those drums speak for me.

It took about a year, but I did get over my fears and learn to enjoy my presentations. In fact, as I got more comfortable, I became more daring. For example, one evening I wanted to say something about the importance of persistence. I thought, *What better example could I possibly use than my seven-year struggle to tie my shoelaces?*

Instead of telling the audience about my struggle, I just showed them. I started my talk with my right foot perched on a stool and my shoelaces untied. I lifted my arms away from my body, allowing everyone to see that I basically had no hands. Then I bent down and silently tied my shoe. When I looked up, I could see tears in the eyes of at least half a dozen people. It was the first time I really thought I could touch people's hearts.

That night I met Kevin and Amity Carriere, a husband and wife who went on to become good friends of mine. They approached me after my "talk" and told me that watching me tie my shoelaces was one of the most inspirational moments they'd ever experienced. I was flattered and thanked them for their kind words. We then began to talk about people who had inspired us throughout our lives.

"Have you ever heard of Wayne Dyer?" Kevin asked.

"Yes, I have," I said with a smile. "I haven't read any of his books, but you're the third person to mention him to me this week."

For me, that was the signal that a new chapter of my life was about to begin.

♦ ♦ ♦

Chapter Twelve

Synchronicity

In the spring of 2004, I arrived at my parents' house for dinner. As I opened the door, I was nearly knocked over by my dad, who rushed toward me and enthusiastically waved a book in my face. "Danny, you've got to read this," he insisted. "Really, you'll love it!"

I think I laughed at his exuberance—as I've said, my father is the even-keeled type. But he was always trying to convince me to read books he'd enjoyed, and since he's a devout Catholic, our tastes are quite different. So I just replied, "Sure, Dad. Whatever."

"No, I'm serious, Danny. This book is so good, it could change your life."

I took a quick glance at the book my father was holding in front of me and saw a very kind-looking man on the cover. I assumed that Dad had picked up a religious book at church in the hopes that I'd read it and start going to Mass again.

Don't get me wrong, I'm certainly not closed off to reading about religion per se—quite the opposite. My friend and former teacher Johnny V had turned me on to all sorts of books dealing with spirituality, and I'd read countless volumes on Eastern religions and philosophy at Loyola University. I just didn't like Christian dogma, since I'd grown up with it and knew it inside out. There were so many other books out there for me to discover that I didn't feel like going over such familiar territory.

"Just leave it for me by the door and I'll take a look at it later," I said to indulge my father, planning to do nothing of the sort. Even though I didn't take the glossy hardcover with me as I left the house that night, I did glance at the cover again on my way out. I saw that the book was called *The Power of Intention,* and it was by a writer I'd never heard of before: Wayne Dyer.

The next night I was at a club in downtown New Orleans, getting ready for a gig. My pal Josh Cooker (Captain Midnight to his friends), the guitarist of the band I was playing with, and I were talking about various things. And then he told me something I certainly didn't expect: "Man, I just read this book I think you would love. It's called *The Power of Intention* by a guy named Wayne Dyer."

"You're kidding me, right?" I shook my head with a smile. "That's like some kind of new Christian thing that just came out, isn't it?"

"No, no, no," he said. "It not about any *one* religion; in a way, it's about all religions. I mean, Dr. Dyer does talk quite a bit about Jesus in the book, but he also talks about

Buddha, the Hindu god Krishna, Mahatma Gandhi, and all sorts of spiritual teachers. It's really insightful and deals with a lot of the stuff you're into, which is why I thought you'd like it."

"Okay, I'll check it out," I promised him.

Two days later, I'd given the Toastmasters presentation where I'd silently tied my shoe, and my new friends Kevin and Amity Carriere approached me and asked if I'd heard of Wayne Dyer. My presentation reminded them of his inspirational new work, *The Power of Intention*. I was amazed by the synchronicity. Both Dad and Josh Cooker had also mentioned this very book to me!

"Have you read it?" Amity wanted to know.

"No, not yet," I answered. "But you can be sure that it just went to the top of my list!"

This was exactly the kind of synchronicity—the experience of two or more unrelated events occurring together in a meaningful manner—that I'd studied in philosophy class and talked about with Johnny V and other well-read, thoughtful people. Hearing about Wayne's book from so many people in my life, and from such vastly different backgrounds, told me that the universe was sending me a message: *Find out who this man is and what he has to say!*

Within a few days, I'd read the book and it blew my mind.

WAYNE DYER HAD A WAY OF EXPLAINING THINGS that I'd been feeling for years but couldn't articulate. So often in my life, my creativity had been driven by a force of will, by fighting *against* things in order to succeed. Sometimes even feeling discriminated against had propelled me forward artistically, so I could prove to myself and others that I was equal to them or better. And although that may have worked for a short time, I learned while studying the philosophy of drumming with Johnny V that the magic of creativity happens when we *open* ourselves to the positive energies of the universe, not the negative.

This was a subject Wayne talked about eloquently in *The Power of Intention*. Intention, he said, is the prime force in the universe that allows an act of true creation to occur. He wrote that we're all spiritual beings connected by a field of energy, and each one of us can tap into that rich and rewarding field when we're open to the universe. When we have the intention to connect, we can co-create our life with all of the positive energy that surrounds us.

So much of this book had taken me back to many wonderful talks I had with Wolf, my dear friend and first spiritual advisor. In the months before he died, we discussed the universal field of energy that connected all living things, which he referred to as the Great Spirit. It now seemed to me that Wayne's book tied together all of the different teachings and philosophies that had inspired me over the years. The result was that I'd been brought to a new level of thinking, feeling, and creativity.

As soon as I finished reading *The Power of Intention,* I called my dad and apologized for being closed off when he had first told me about it. I also thanked Kevin and Amity for suggesting I read Wayne's book. And I was so thankful to Josh that for months after he first mentioned *The Power of Intention* to me, he and I teased each other by calling one another "Wayne" whenever we met up.

After Katrina and my return home from Brooklyn, I found myself devouring just about everything Wayne Dyer had written, and I began to incorporate the principles he wrote about into my everyday life, and the results were remarkable. My music career, which was already doing well, reached a new level—now that I was back in New Orleans, I was attracting more gigs and playing with more bands than ever before. But unlike what had happened in the past, the hard work and long hours weren't tiring me out. It was actually having the opposite effect: I had tons of energy to spare at the end of even the toughest day. I also became so relaxed and confident as a public speaker that I was asked to become president of my local chapter of Toastmasters.

I found it so incredible that in just a few short years, I'd gone from being a terrified and reluctant guy who hung back in the shadows while speaking publicly, to a competent and effective inspirational speaker. I could hardly believe that these days I was addressing groups as large as 1,000.

Now, I'm not saying that all of this was because of Wayne, but reading his books *did* help me expand upon my passion—like believing I could play the drums when people told me I couldn't—and apply it to every facet of my life.

IN APRIL 2008, I WAS PLAYING WITH A BAND called Spyboy during the annual New Orleans Jazz & Heritage Festival, one of the largest music festivals in the country. The festival keeps just about every musician in the region working day and night for two solid weeks, which is great. During a rare night off I called up my pal Benny, the Spyboy guitarist, and invited him to join me for dinner at a new pizza place downtown.

Now ever since I'd been introduced to *The Power of Intention* three times in one week back in 2004, I'd been looking out for other synchronicities that might crop up in my life. As I've said, I believe that synchronicity is one way the universe tells us to pay attention to what's going on around us. So when Benny told me he was already going to that particular pizza parlor to meet his friend Tiffany, I figured synchronicity was telling me I had to go as well. Coincidentally, Benny told me that Tiffany lived on the Hawaiian island of Maui. Since I knew that Wayne Dyer also just happened to reside in Maui, I thought, *Aha! Another case of synchronicity! Better keep your eyes and ears open, Dan!*

We met up at the restaurant, and Benny introduced me to Tiffany. She was a very open and direct young woman whom I liked instantly, and we all felt at ease with one another right away.

Somehow it came up in conversation that Tiffany had met an older gentleman at a yoga class in Maui who'd asked her to work for him as his assistant.

"Oh, really," I replied with a smile. "Would this gentleman happen to be an author?"

"Yes, how did you know that?"

"Would he happen to be a best-selling author?"

"Yes, Dan, he would. He's written lots of books and does television specials," Tiffany said. "You're freaking me out a bit."

"And would his name happen to be Wayne Dyer?" I asked, knowing that the universe was knocking at my door yet again.

"How did you know that? Do you know Wayne?"

"I've read all his books," I explained, "but I haven't met him . . . *yet.*"

As the evening progressed, I told Tiffany all about my accident and how Wayne's books had helped inspire me to try to become an inspirational speaker just like he was. My new friend was shocked by the coincidence— but *I* knew it wasn't a coincidence at all. She went on to say she was sure that Wayne would love to meet me and hear my story. So before we said good night, she asked for my phone number and promised to call as soon as she'd spoken to Wayne about me.

Several weeks passed, and sure enough, Tiffany called from Hawaii to say that Wayne definitely wanted to meet me. She said that he'd be speaking in Florida in the fall, and if I could get to Tampa in October, she'd arrange a meeting.

"Sign me up," I told her. "I'll see you in Tampa!"

I immediately picked up the phone and called my friend Kevin from Toastmasters because he and his wife Amity were such fans of Wayne. "Guess what?!" I announced. "I've just been invited to go to Florida and meet Wayne Dyer!"

"No way!" Kevin exclaimed. "You won't believe what I'm doing right now—I'm listening to Wayne Dyer's CD *The Secrets of the Power of Intention!* Is that synchronicity or what?"

I definitely took that as another sign from the universe. In fact, I figured I'd better invite Kevin to come to Tampa with me and meet Wayne.

That October, my friend and I walked off a plane in Florida and set out to meet our mentor. Unfortunately, Wayne had an emergency appointment and had to cancel our meeting, but Kevin and I went to his presentation— and, of course, we were completely inspired. The next day we went to Wayne's book signing. Kevin, bless his heart, went up to Wayne, pointed me out, and told him who I was.

Wayne told us to hang around for a while, and eventually sent his assistant to bring us backstage before his next presentation. Even though Tiffany had told Wayne all about me, he asked more questions about my life, and we talked for quite a while. When it came time to say good-bye, he looked me in the eye and said, very seriously, "Listen to me, Dan. You have an important story to tell that can inspire thousands and thousands of people. You must tell your story to the world, and I'm going to help you do just that. I want you to join me onstage, and that's when you can begin."

I couldn't believe my ears. I'd been reading Wayne's books, listening to his CDs, and trying to emulate his inspirational speaking style . . . and now he was asking me to join him onstage! What more proof did I need that the power of intention was truly a wonderful force in the universe?

WAYNE INVITED ME TO BE PART OF his upcoming presentation the following month in Phoenix, Arizona. When the big weekend finally arrived, I met him at his hotel before the show. I'm sure he could see that, although I'd played drums on stages across the country, I was as nervous as could be.

"Don't worry," he said, putting me at ease. "You're going to be great. Just tell your story from your heart and play your music from the heart—trust me, you'll be fine!" How could I *not* trust him; he was Wayne Dyer!

The next morning a new life began for me. I sat in the audience listening as Wayne talked about me to the thousands of people who'd come to see and hear *him!* He told them how I'd been burned, and the journey I'd been on since leaving the Shriners hospital so long ago. He told my story in such an emotional and powerful way that I teared up myself.

Finally, he said, "Ladies and gentlemen, I give you Dan Caro."

Any nervousness I had vanished when I walked on that stage with Wayne. I fell into my story, and before I knew it, I was playing the drums. When it was over, I was standing in the center of the stage basking in the glow of a standing ovation, feeling completely surrounded by the warmth and support of thousands of beautiful, loving people.

Since then I've appeared with Wayne onstage many times and have even taken part in a special for public television based on his book *Excuses Begone!* One of the most special moments for me came when Wayne introduced my parents to the audience, and I saw that Mom and Dad were beaming with pride at how far I'd come. That show has since been viewed by hundreds of thousands of people, and I continue to receive letters and calls from all kinds of folks who say that hearing my story and watching me play the drums helped them deal with their own particular hardships.

Thanks to Wayne, my career as an inspirational speaker has taken off, and I'm now telling my story to groups all over America. The core message I share is this: if we live our lives in the light of love and positive energy, then no matter what happens to us or what challenges we face from day to day or year to year, we can experience life as a precious gift.

My gift has been living a full and happy existence after being burned beyond recognition as a child. This gift of fire is one that I have learned how to share with others—one that I hope to continue to share for many years to come.

◆ ◆ ◆

Acknowledgments

This Divine universe has gifted me with some very wonderful people in my life. I'd like to offer my thanks and love to them.

To my mother, Marilyn: You were my voice and my guide for many years in the hospital, as well as my protector from those who tried to harm me through their ignorant and vicious comments and actions when I was too young to fend for myself. The love you've shown me is unparalleled. Thank you for always being there for me. You are the strongest person I've ever known. I love you very much.

To my father, John: You are a pillar of virtue. Your faith, wisdom, and guidance are responsible for my strength and independence. I could not have come as far in life as I have without your love and support. I thank you for the values you have instilled in me. I love you.

To my brothers: Johnny, I've looked to you as a guide for living. You have inspired me, and I'm grateful that you are in my life. Scott, I've always admired your individuality and intelligence. We have shared some unforgettable experiences, and I'm honored to be your brother. Paul, you have been one of my greatest teachers and best friends. I'm humbled to be your brother.

To Dr. Wayne Dyer: The way we were brought together is a miracle in itself. You have influenced and inspired millions, and I'm glad to be among them. As though divinely inspired, you appeared in my life at just the right time. My gratitude goes beyond words. Thank you for your friendship and for introducing me to Hay House.

To Tiffany Saia: You have blessed me with your friendship and a gift I'm unable to pay back. Instead, I choose to pay it forward and offer my story to all who will read or listen. Introducing me to Wayne has changed my life. You are a wonderful and beautiful person. God bless you.

To Reid Tracy: Thank you for believing in me and giving me the opportunity to help inspire a great number of people. I hope that together we can reach a vast audience and teach them that life is a gift and something to be grateful for.

To Jill Kramer, Shannon Littrell, Christy Salinas, Amy Rose Grigoriou, Riann Bender, Stacey Smith, and the staff at Hay House: Thank you for your patience and help while working with Steve and me on this project. To Hay House's Events Director, Nancy Levin, thank you for your assistance and patience with me.

To the Shriners of North America and the doctors and staff of the Shriners Hospitals for Children: To you, I literally owe my life. I have spent some of my greatest days with you recovering from surgeries or in physical therapy, and currently as an ambassador for your wonderful organization. Each of you is a godsend. You'll never truly realize all that you've done for nearly one million children and their families. On behalf of all of them, I thank you.

To my friends Kevin and Amity Carriere, to whom I am deeply indebted: When we met at a Toastmasters meeting in 2004, I couldn't have imagined the road we would travel together. Thank you for believing in me and introducing me to the work of Wayne Dyer. I could not have come this far without your selfless advice and support. I love you both very much.

And to my new friend and co-author, Steve Erwin: I believe that no other person could have helped write my story with such intensity and passion. When Wayne and Reid told me that you were interested in working with me on this book, all of my fears about being a first-time author were put to rest. You are a tremendously gifted writer, and proof of that is how you bring words to life. Thank you, and I look forward to a long friendship and hopefully a few more collaborations.

— **Dan Caro**

♦ ♦

Thank you, Dan, for trusting me to bring words to your inspiring story. To the Hay House gang—Reid Tracy, Jill Kramer, Shannon Littrell, Christy Salinas, and Riann Bender—thank you for your patience and faith, as always. To Dwayne Raymond, a friend and a fine writer, thanks for all your help and hard work. And to my wife, Natasha, who knows all about destiny and following one's dreams . . . thanks for always being there.

— **Steve Erwin**

♦ ♦ ♦

About the Authors

When he was two years old, **Dan Caro** was engulfed in the flames of a gasoline explosion in his family garage. The accident left him with third-degree burns over 80 percent of his body and forever altered the course of his life.

But at a very early age, Dan vowed that his injuries would never determine his potential or put limits on his dreams. When he was 12, he began playing the drums despite the loss of his hands. He uses his left thumb to grip one drumstick and attaches the other stick to his right wrist with rubber bands. With this simple device, Dan became a highly respected drummer in his home-town of New Orleans.

In recent years, Dan has also become an inspirational speaker, sharing his personal story with audiences across the country to illustrate that the only limits we face in life are the ones we place on ourselves.

In addition to his music and speaking career, Dan serves as an ambassador for the Shriners of North America.

You can learn more about him by visiting: **www.dancaro.com**.

◆ ◆

Steve Erwin is a Toronto-born writer and award-winning journalist working in the print and broadcast media. He co-authored the *New York Times* best-selling memoir, *Left to Tell: Discovering God Amidst the Rwandan Holocaust* and two follow-up books in the series—*Led by Faith: Rising from the Ashes of the Rwandan Genocide* and *Our Lady of Kibeho: Mary Speaks to the World from the Heart of Africa*. He lives in Manhattan with his wife, journalist and author Natasha Stoynoff.

◆ ◆ ◆

Hay House Titles of Related Interest

LIVING THROUGH THE RACKET:
How I Survived Leukemia . . . and Rediscovered My Self,
by Corina Morariu, with Allen Rucker

THE POWER OF INTENTION:
Learning to Co-create Your World Your Way,
by Dr. Wayne W. Dyer

THE PRIEST AND THE MEDIUM:
The Amazing True Story of Psychic Medium B. Anne
Gehman and Her Husband, Former Jesuit Priest Wayne
Knoll, Ph.D., by Suzanne Giesemann

THE SHIFT:
Taking Your Life from Ambition to Meaning,
by Dr. Wayne W. Dyer

THE SPONTANEOUS HEALING OF BELIEF:
Shattering the Paradigm of False Limits,
by Gregg Braden

♦ ♦

All of the above are available at your local bookstore,
or may be ordered by visiting:

Hay House USA: **www.hayhouse.com**®
Hay House Australia: **www.hayhouse.com.au**
Hay House UK: **www.hayhouse.co.uk**
Hay House South Africa: **www.hayhouse.co.za**
Hay House India: **www.hayhouse.co.in**

We hope you enjoyed this Hay House book.
If you'd like to receive our online catalog featuring
additional information on Hay House books and products,
or if you'd like to find out more about the
Hay Foundation, please contact:

Hay House, Inc., P.O. Box 5100, Carlsbad, CA 92018-5100

(760) 431-7695 or **(800) 654-5126**
(760) 431-6948 (fax) or **(800) 650-5115 (fax)**
www.hayhouse.com® • **www.hayfoundation.org**

♦ ♦

Published and distributed in Australia by:
Hay House Australia Pty. Ltd., 18/36 Ralph St.,
Alexandria NSW 2015 • *Phone:* 612-9669-4299
Fax: 612-9669-4144 • www.hayhouse.com.au

Published and distributed in the United Kingdom by:
Hay House UK, Ltd., 292B Kensal Rd.,
London W10 5BE • *Phone:* 44-20-8962-1230
Fax: 44-20-8962-1239 • www.hayhouse.co.uk

Published and distributed in the Republic of South Africa by:
Hay House SA (Pty), Ltd., P.O. Box 990,
Witkoppen 2068 • *Phone/Fax:* 27-11-467-8904
info@hayhouse.co.za • www.hayhouse.co.za

Published in India by:
Hay House Publishers India, Muskaan Complex, Plot No. 3,
B-2, Vasant Kunj, New Delhi 110 070 • *Phone:* 91-11-4176-
1620 • *Fax:* 91-11-4176-1630 • www.hayhouse.co.in

Distributed in Canada by:
Raincoast, 9050 Shaughnessy St., Vancouver,
B.C. V6P 6E5 • *Phone:* (604) 323-7100 • *Fax:*
(604) 323-2600 • www.raincoast.com

♦ ♦

Take Your Soul on a Vacation

Visit **www.HealYourLife.com®** to regroup, recharge,
and reconnect with your own magnificence.
Featuring blogs, mind-body-spirit news, and life-changing
wisdom from Louise Hay and friends.

Visit **www.HealYourLife.com** today!

Mind Your Body,
Mend Your Spirit

Hay House is the ultimate resource for inspirational and health-conscious books, audio programs, movies, events, e-newsletters, member communities, and much more.

Visit **www.hayhouse.com**® today and nourish your soul.

UPLIFTING EVENTS
Join your favorite authors at live events in a city near you or log on to **www.hayhouse.com** to visit with Hay House authors online during live, interactive Web events.

INSPIRATIONAL RADIO
Daily inspiration while you're at work or at home. Enjoy radio programs featuring your favorite authors, streaming live on the Internet 24/7 at **HayHouseRadio.com**®. Tune in and tune up your spirit!

VIP STATUS
Join the Hay House VIP membership program today and enjoy exclusive discounts on books, CDs, calendars, card decks, and more. You'll also receive 10% off all event reservations (excluding cruises). Visit **www.hayhouse.com/wisdom** to join the Hay House Wisdom Community™.

Visit **www.hayhouse.com** and enter priority code 2723
during checkout for special savings!
(One coupon per customer.)